YOGI
MAHA
METHOD

ISBN: 979-8-9896889-5-1
Imprint: Independently published
(Paperback)

Library of Congress Catalog Card Number: 0000-0000
Copyright © 2024 by Yogi Maha Method

Maha Bodhi (Author)
Tiffany Yau (Designer, Editor)

This book is dedicated to the incredible teachers who inspired my journey to become a yoga instructor and to every single yoga student who has ever walked into my class. Your presence and dedication have touched my heart and continues to guide me on this incredible journey.

Table of Contents

Externally Rotated Standing Poses

Inversions and Arm Balances

FOREWORD

When I first started the 200-hour yoga teacher training with Maha Bodhi in her first cohort of students, I was seeking something to fully immerse myself in something that brought me joy while navigating a difficult period in my life. While excited to deepen my practice and learn more about the cultural richness of yoga, I truly gained so much more. As Maha often says, "We don't practice yoga to get better at yoga. We practice yoga to get better at living life." This book encapsulates the thoughtfulness, intention, and compassion that shines through Maha's teaching style, and I am thrilled for others to benefit from this work.

I am incredibly grateful and honored to write this foreword and edit this book. As someone who could barely touch my toes before the training, the idea of becoming a yoga instructor seemed insurmountable. However, I discovered that yoga is so much more than mastering physical poses. It is a holistic practice that embraces inclusivity, self-acceptance, and a deep connection to one's inner self.

One of the most beautiful yet underrated aspects I've learned to appreciate through Maha is that yoga is one of the few workouts where you can truly show up as you are. It embraces inclusivity with no one-size-fits-all approach. It doesn't matter if you're a seasoned athlete or a beginner, young or old, flexible or not. There is no judgment, competition, or pressure to perform at a certain level—yoga offers modifications tailored to individual abilities and needs. The magic often lies in the quality of the instructor.

Contrary to popular belief, being a good yoga instructor requires more than knowledge, cueing, or flexibility. A great instructor honors and educates students on the significance of yoga and its rich historical and cultural roots. But an exceptional instructor encourages you to listen to your body, honor your limitations, focus on your personal growth, and foster love, kindness, and compassion in all aspects of life—lessons I am fortunate to have learned through Maha.

Under her wing, I learned that yoga isn't about touching your toes but what you learn on the way down, and sometimes we'll need to learn how to fall to find our balance. To be able to hold the seat of the teacher and cultivate that kind of space for individuals, welcoming all with open arms, is truly so special.

As you embark on this journey of studying yoga and teaching, I encourage you to approach it with an open mind and heart. The lessons contained within these pages have the power to shape not only your practice and teaching but perhaps also aspects of your life you never foresaw possible. I am thrilled for you to embark on this path of self-discovery and can't wait to see how yoga will enrich your world as you enrich the worlds of others.

- Tiffany Yau

INTRODUCTION

"Yoga is the journey of the self, through the self, to the self." - The Bhagavad Gita.

This ancient wisdom perfectly encapsulates the essence of yoga, a practice that goes beyond the physical to touch every aspect of our being.

After surviving a brutal upbringing in Yemen, where I was enslaved as a female, forced into arranged marriages twice, faced multiple life-threatening situations, and endured two civil wars, I eventually arrived in the U.S. and was later diagnosed with cancer. Yoga has been my anchor, a sacred space where I learned to let my light shine and be all that I am. My purpose now is to share this gift, to hold space for others to transform, and to pass along the yogic teachings I've gathered throughout the years. This book is a part of that mission.

My journey into yoga began in the most humbling way. My first class was not just challenging; it was downright brutal. After years of neglecting my body and avoiding physical activity, I found myself struggling to keep up. During this first class, I got so sick that I had to roll up my yoga mat and sneak out the back of the class to leave within the first ten minutes. To add to my embarrassment, the class was taught by the iconic yoga teacher and inventor of power yoga Bryan Kest.

That initial mortifying experience at Kest's class planted a seed deep within my consciousness. I saw the glow on the faces of seasoned yogis, the serene and awakened look that spoke of a life experienced differently. I yearned for that same inner peace and strength. So, I made a commitment to myself—I didn't give up. I kept showing up, class after class, gradually growing stronger and finding my way into the flow, the elusive "yoga zone." It wasn't easy, and it certainly didn't happen overnight. Yoga is, after all, a practice. It required dedication, patience, and most importantly, compassion toward myself.

There's a saying, "When the student is ready, the teacher appears." Over a decade of devoted practice, I was fortunate to study with celebrity yoga instructors like Travis Eliot and Lauren Eckstrom, earning my Yoga Alliance instructor certificate. I remember my first day in yoga teacher training vividly. Travis asked me to introduce myself, and I said, "Hi, my name is Maha." He then asked, "Do you want to share with everyone what Maha means?" I explained, "It means 'big beautiful eyes.' It's a common name in Yemen, where I am originally from." Travis smiled and added, "'Maha' also means 'the great' in Sanskrit, which is the ancient language of yoga." At that moment, everyone in the room looked at me with a gaze that seemed to recognize "You were destined to be a yogi." It was then I knew I had arrived, that I had finally found my home and place in the world. I realized my life would never be the same, and I was right.

Life has a way of coming full circle, as I eventually ended up teaching yoga at Bryan Kest's world-renowned yoga studio, Santa Monica Power Yoga. Later on, Kest, as a featured guest trainer, joined Yogi Maha Method teacher training that I developed. I stood on prestigious stages and led inspirational speaking engagements, hosted five-star international yoga retreats, and special events for Fortune 500 corporations. I was honored to be featured in the HBO documentary "Scars Unseen." Alongside incredible women like Michelle Obama and Serena Williams, I became represented by the Harry Walker Agency in Beverly Hills, California, and I continue to strive to inspire and empower others through my work.

This book is designed to guide you through the intricate path of becoming a yoga teacher. Whether you are at the beginning of your yoga journey or looking to deepen your practice and understanding, this book offers comprehensive insights into the philosophy, practice, and teaching methodology of yoga. In this book, you will find detailed discussions on the history and philosophy of yoga, practical advice on developing your personal practice, step-by-step instructions on key asanas, and essential teaching techniques. We will also explore the business aspects of becoming a yoga teacher and tips for fostering a supportive community.

Take your time to absorb each section, practice the exercises, and reflect on the insights shared. This book is both a guide and a companion on your teaching journey. Yoga is a continuous learning experience, and this book aims to support you every step of the way. Embarking on the path of a yoga teacher is a deeply rewarding experience that will not only transform your own life but also touch the lives of countless others.

You will find a journey that challenges you physically and inspires you mentally, emotionally, and spiritually. Embrace this journey with curiosity, dedication, and joy. My teachings are designed to help you heal, transform, and ultimately, manifest your best life. So, roll out your yoga mat, open your heart, and get ready to embark on a transformative journey.

Welcome to your practice. Welcome to your transformation. Welcome to the beginning of your best life.

Maha Bodhi, M.A.

THE HISTORY OF YOGA

THE HISTORY OF YOGA

Definition of Yoga

The definition of the word "yoga" itself is derived from the Sanskrit word "yuj," meaning to unite or to join.

The goal of yoga, as outlined by the ancient sage Patañjali in the Yoga Sūtras, is defined in the opening aphorism as: yogaś citta-vṛtti-nirodhaḥ. This is commonly translated as "Yoga is the cessation of the fluctuations of the mind." In this context, citta refers to the mind-field as a whole, including thoughts, emotions, memories, and perceptions, while vṛttis are the movements or patterns that arise within it. Nirodhaḥ means restraint, quieting, or cessation. Patañjali immediately follows this with the next sūtra: tadā draṣṭuḥ svarūpe'vasthānam. Then, the seer abides in its own true nature. So together "Yoga is the cessation of the fluctuations of the mind. Then, the seer abides in its own true nature." When mental activity quiets, awareness rests in its natural clarity. This state is not created, but revealed as agitation subsides.

Patanjali, credited with developing the Yoga Sutras, is traditionally regarded as a historical human figure. However, due to the lack of concrete historical evidence and the mythological elements surrounding his life, some consider him to be a semi-mythical or legendary figure, and is honored as a great sage and scholar who systematized and codified the practices of yoga into the Yoga Sutras. While the exact details of Patanjali's life and the historical accuracy of his existence remain unclear, his contributions to yoga through the Yoga Sutras are widely recognized and respected. Whether viewed as a historical figure or a semi-mythical one, Patanjali's impact on the tradition of yoga is profound and enduring.

Yoga Philosophy and Ancient Texts

The classical form of yoga, as outlined in the Yoga Sutras of Patanjali, dates back to around 200 BCE to 200 CE. Patanjali's text provided a systematic framework for practicing yoga, outlining the eight limbs of yoga, which include ethical guidelines, physical postures (asanas), breath control (pranayama), and meditation techniques.

The history of yoga is ancient and intricate, intertwining with the cultural, spiritual, and philosophical traditions of India. While the exact origins of yoga are debated, its roots can be traced back to ancient Indian civilization, with the earliest mentions in sacred texts known as the "vedas", a collection of sacred texts dating back over 5,000 years.

Initially, yoga practices were developed to support spiritual insight and self-realization, not physical fitness.

Thousands of years ago, yogis would meditate within the caves of isolated mountains for extended periods, sometimes days or even months, sustaining themselves with just one meal a month. However, due to prolonged stillness, their bodies would become stiff. It was then that they began incorporating physical postures to stretch their bodies and stimulate blood flow. Therefore, the primary goal of their physical practice was to enable them to sustain meditation for longer periods.

Hatha Yoga

Throughout history, various schools of yoga emerged, each emphasizing different aspects of the practice. The word "Hatha" translates to "force" or "effort" in Sanskrit. It's derived from the combination of two Sanskrit words: "ha," meaning "sun," and "tha," meaning "moon." In the context of yoga, "Hatha" represents the union of opposites or the balance of polar energies, emphasizing the harmonization of physical and mental aspects through the practice of postures (asanas) and breath control (pranayama). Hatha yoga, which focuses on physical postures and breath control, gained prominence in the Middle Ages. Most popular power yoga and vinyasa yoga styles that are practiced today fall under the category of Hatha yoga. Any yoga practice that incorporates poses (asana) is considered Hatha yoga.

In the late 19th and early 20th centuries, yoga experienced a revival with the efforts of Indian yoga masters like Paramahansa Yogananda (1893–1952), who was a spiritual teacher and yogi who played a significant role in popularizing yoga and meditation in the West, particularly through his book "Autobiography of a Yogi." Yogananda founded the Self-Realization Fellowship (SRF) in 1920 in Los Angeles.

In the 20th century, yoga continued to gain widespread popularity in the West, fueled by the interest in Eastern spirituality, alternative medicine, and holistic health practices. Figures like B.K.S. Iyengar, K. Pattabhi Jois, and Swami Sivananda further popularized different styles of yoga, such as Iyengar yoga, Ashtanga yoga, and Sivananda yoga.

History & Lineage of Yogi Maha Method

Bryan Kest, who had a profound impact on my yoga teaching journey as my first yoga instructor, initially studied Ashtanga yoga with Pattabhi Jois. He later developed and founded what is now one of the most popular styles of yoga, known as power yoga or sometimes called vinyasa yoga, and became known as the inventor of power yoga.

Kest's teaching style played a pivotal role and inspired me to create my own teaching method, Yogi Maha Method. Later on, I pursued further studies with world-renowned yoga instructors Travis Eliot and Lauren Ekstrom, both of whom were mentored by Kest. The Yogi Method is a strong physical flow that strengthens the body, creative in its artful sequencing yet rooted in yoga tradition. It fosters an experience of transcendence, guiding practitioners to move beyond the physical realm and drop into a deeper state of consciousness. This journey into deeper awareness aligns with the ultimate goal of ancient yoga practice: the transcendence of the body and the realization of higher states of consciousness.

Yogi Maha Method School Lineage: Maha Bodhi => Travis Eliot => Srivatsa Ramaswami => B. K. S. Iyengar => Krishnamacharya

Today, yoga is practiced by millions of people worldwide, encompassing a diverse array of styles, from the physically demanding power yoga to the gentle, meditative practices of yin yoga and restorative yoga. While modern yoga may vary widely in its approach and emphasis, its underlying goal remains consistent: to cultivate self-awareness, inner peace, and spiritual growth.

Yoga Styles and Traditions

Rāja Yoga

Rāja Yoga, often referred to as the "royal path," is the system of yoga articulated in Patañjali's Yoga Sūtras. It emphasizes mastery of the mind through ethical discipline, self-regulation, concentration, meditation, and absorption. Its purpose is the cessation of mental fluctuations so that awareness can rest in its own nature. Rāja Yoga provides the philosophical and meditative foundation of the yoga path.

Haṭha Yoga

Haṭha Yoga is a practical system that uses the body, breath, and subtle techniques to prepare the system for meditation. It includes āsana, prāṇāyāma, bandhas, mudrās, and cleansing practices. Rather than being an end in itself, Haṭha Yoga aims to regulate prāṇa, balance opposing forces, and stabilize the body and nervous system so higher states of awareness can arise naturally.

Tantra Yoga

Tantra Yoga is a broad spiritual framework that views the body, senses, and world as valid instruments for awakening rather than obstacles to transcendence. It works skillfully with mantra, visualization, ritual, and subtle anatomy to transform experience rather than reject it. In tantra, the body is understood as a sacred field through which consciousness can recognize itself when energy and awareness are integrated.

Karma Yoga

Karma Yoga is the path of selfless action. It emphasizes engaging fully in life while relinquishing attachment to outcomes. Through conscious action performed without egoic grasping, habitual identification weakens and clarity deepens. Karma Yoga transforms everyday activity into a means of purification and liberation.

Bhakti Yoga

Bhakti Yoga is the path of devotion and relationship. It cultivates love, surrender, and reverence toward the divine through practices such as chanting, prayer, ritual, and remembrance. Bhakti Yoga softens the ego and opens the heart, allowing emotional energy to be refined into devotion and trust.

Kundalini Yoga

Kundalini Yoga is a practice-based approach that uses kriyā, structured sequences of movement coordinated with breath, along with chanting and meditation. These practices are designed to regulate the nervous system, refine awareness, and support the gradual reorganization of energy within the body. In yogic symbolism, kuṇḍalinī is often represented as a coiled serpent, not as a force to be awakened aggressively, but as a metaphor for potential awareness becoming conscious of itself.

Modern Yoga Styles

These are yoga styles commonly found in yoga studios throughout the United States today.

Power Yoga

Power yoga is a physically demanding, fitness-oriented style of yoga that emphasizes strength, endurance, and sustained intensity. Classes are typically fast-paced, linking poses together with breath to build heat and challenge the body. While breath is used to support movement, the primary focus is on physical conditioning rather than breath-led flow or traditional sequencing.

Vinyasa Yoga

Vinyasa yoga is characterized by fluid transitions between postures that are guided by the rhythm of the breath. Sequences often include sun salutations, standing poses, balances, and occasional inversions. Intensity can vary widely, but breath coordination and smooth transitions are central, making vinyasa distinct from power yoga's emphasis on exertion.

Gentle Yoga

Gentle yoga is a slower-paced style designed to support ease, accessibility, and relaxation. It emphasizes simple postures, longer holds, and mindful breathing, making it suitable for beginners, individuals recovering from injury, or those seeking a calming practice. The focus is on comfort, awareness, and gentle movement rather than physical challenge.

Yin Yoga

Yin yoga is a slow-paced practice that emphasizes long-held postures, typically seated or reclining, designed to place gentle stress on connective tissues such as fascia, ligaments, and joints. Poses are usually held for several minutes, allowing the body to soften gradually and encouraging stillness and introspection. Yin yoga supports joint mobility, patience, and deep awareness, and differs from gentle yoga in that it intentionally works with sustained holds rather than comfort alone.

Restorative Yoga

Restorative yoga is a deeply restful practice focused entirely on relaxation and recovery. Unlike yin yoga, restorative poses involve no stretching or effort. The body is fully supported with props so that muscles can relax completely. Poses are held for extended periods, allowing the nervous system to settle and the body to rest. This style is suitable for all levels and is often used to support stress reduction, recovery, and deep rest.

Chair Yoga

Chair yoga is an accessible form of yoga practiced seated or using a chair for support. It adapts traditional yoga movements and breathing practices to make them available to people with limited mobility or those who prefer a gentler approach. Chair yoga is commonly offered in workplaces, senior centers, and rehabilitation settings, and emphasizes posture, breath awareness, and ease of movement.

AcroYoga

AcroYoga is a partner-based practice that blends elements of yoga, acrobatics, and Thai massage. It involves cooperative movement where participants take on roles such as base, flyer, and spotter. AcroYoga emphasizes communication, trust, and coordination while exploring strength, balance, and playfulness in a shared practice.

Aerial Yoga

Aerial yoga is a style of yoga that uses suspended fabric hammocks to support the body. The hammock assists with balance, supports inversions, and allows practitioners to explore poses with reduced load on joints. Aerial yoga offers a different physical experience from mat-based yoga and combines strength, flexibility, and spatial awareness in a supported environment.

THE SUBTLE BODY

THE SUBTLE BODY

Yoga Subtle Anatomy

Yoga subtle anatomy refers to the non-physical dimensions of the human system as described in yogic philosophy and practice. While the physical body can be observed and studied through anatomy, yoga recognizes subtler layers of organization that shape how the body, mind, and perception function together. These subtle aspects are not visible through dissection, yet their effects are experienced through patterns of vitality, emotion, attention, and consciousness.

From the yogic perspective, systems such as the chakras, nāḍīs, prāṇa vāyus, kośas, and bandhas describe how life experience is organized and regulated within the human being. Although a surgeon cannot directly see a chakra or a nāḍī, patterns of balance or imbalance in these subtle systems are reflected in physiological function, psychological states, and habitual ways of relating to life.

Working skillfully with subtle anatomy does not mean forcing energy or attempting to "activate" structures, but rather learning to regulate breath, attention, and movement so the system can organize itself more coherently. Practices such as āsana, prāṇāyāma, meditation, mantra, and contemplative inquiry support this process by stabilizing prāṇa and refining perception.

The phrase "where attention goes, energy flows" points to the intimate relationship between awareness and prāṇa. Attention does not create energy, but it influences how prāṇa organizes and moves within the system. When awareness is placed steadily and without strain on a particular region or function of the subtle body, perception deepens and regulation naturally improves.

Through practices such as meditation, breath awareness, and mindful observation, sensitivity to subtle patterns increases. For example, placing attention at the heart center does not force emotional change, but it may allow patterns related to connection, openness, or contraction to be seen more clearly and reorganize naturally. In this way, awareness becomes a tool for regulation rather than control, allowing the subtle anatomy to function with greater clarity, balance, and integration.

As awareness becomes steadier, patterns that once felt blocked or stagnant are no longer reinforced through unconscious habit. Rather than actively trying to clear or manipulate energy, the simple act of sustained observation allows tension, emotional contraction, and energetic congestion to reorganize naturally. In the same way, bringing mindful attention to the breath and the movement of prāṇa supports regulation, vitality, and ease by stabilizing the system rather than forcing change.

The power of placing conscious awareness on any aspect of the subtle body lies in the inherent interconnectedness of body, breath, mind, and perception. Attention does not impose healing, but it reveals patterns clearly enough for them to resolve on their own. As this skill matures, self-awareness deepens, balance increases, and vitality becomes more stable. In this way, yoga emphasizes conscious participation in one's own integration and awakening, not through control or effort, but through clarity, presence, and discernment.

The Maha Bhutas

In the yogic tradition, the mahābhūtas are the five great elements that describe how manifestation unfolds from subtle to gross. These elements are earth (pṛthvī), water (apas), fire (tejas), air (vāyu), and space (ākāśa). They are not merely physical substances, but organizing principles that shape both the material world and human experience.

Classical yogic cosmology describes creation as emerging from subtle vibration, symbolized by Oṁ. From this subtle field arises space (ākāśa), which provides the condition for movement. From space emerges air (vāyu), representing motion and vitality. Movement generates heat, giving rise to fire (tejas), which enables transformation. Fire condenses into water (apas), allowing cohesion and flow, and water further solidifies into earth (pṛthvī), forming stable structure. This progression describes the movement from subtle potential into tangible form.

Within the human system, the mahābhūtas express themselves through the body, breath, perception, and patterns of experience. They do not exist as isolated components but function together through prāṇa and its directional movements. Imbalance in elemental expression reflects dysregulation of prāṇa rather than a literal excess or deficiency of an element.

Earth (Prithvi)

Represents stability, structure, and groundedness. In the body it is expressed through bones, tissues, and physical form, and is primarily reflected through the mūlādhāra chakra and the annamaya kośa. When earth is coherently expressed, there is steadiness and trust. When disturbed, experience may be dominated by fear, rigidity, or insecurity.

Water (Apas)

Represents fluidity, adaptability, and emotional movement. It is expressed through bodily fluids and relational flow, and is reflected through the svādhiṣṭhāna chakra. When water is coherent, emotions move naturally. When disturbed, experience may swing between suppression and overwhelm.

Fire (Agni)

Represents transformation, digestion, and clarity. It governs metabolic processes and the digestion of both food and experience. Fire is reflected most clearly through the maṇipūra chakra, where identity, agency, and momentum are organized. When coherent, there is clarity and appropriate action. When disturbed, experience may manifest as control, anxiety, or collapse.

Air (Vayu)

Represents movement, exchange, and relational connection. It is expressed through breath, circulation, and emotional resonance, and is reflected through the anāhata chakra. When air is coherent, connection is present without attachment. When disturbed, experience may feel scattered, withdrawn, or unstable.

Space (Akasha)

Represents openness, resonance, and the field in which all experience occurs. It is reflected through the viśuddha chakra and relates to expression, listening, and clarity. When space is coherent, communication is clear and receptive. When disturbed, expression may feel blocked or disconnected.

In yoga, the aim is not to manipulate or balance the elements directly, but to regulate prāṇa so that elemental expressions organize themselves naturally. As breath, attention, and movement become coherent, the mahābhūtas express themselves in harmony, supporting physical health, psychological balance, and clarity of perception.

The chakras are functional centers of organization within the subtle body where physical, emotional, psychological, and perceptual experience tends to organize. They are functioning at all times. When prāṇa vāyus are regulated and coordinated, the chakras reorganize naturally and function coherently. Each chakra corresponds to a particular domain of human experience and is traditionally associated with one of the mahābhūtas (elements). Colors and bīja mantras are used as symbolic supports for awareness, not as tools for activation

Root Chakra (Muladhara Chakra)

Is associated with stability, grounding, and survival. It corresponds to the earth element and is located at the base of the spine. Its traditional color is red, symbolizing solidity and grounding, and it is associated with the mahābhūta earth (pṛthvī), with the bīja mantra LAM. This center organizes experiences related to safety, belonging, physical stability, and basic human needs such as shelter, food, money, and bodily security. It influences the legs, feet, bones, and pelvic floor. When this center functions coherently, there is a felt sense of stability and trust in life. When disorganized, experience may be dominated by fear, scarcity, or chronic insecurity.

Sacral Chakra (Svadhisthana Chakra)

Is associated with fluidity, sensation, and emotional movement. It corresponds to the water element and is located in the lower abdomen. Its traditional color is orange, symbolizing flow and creativity, and it is associated with the mahābhūta water (apas), with the bīja mantra VAM. This center organizes experiences related to pleasure, emotion, intimacy, creativity, and relational flow. It influences the reproductive organs, kidneys, and bladder. When functioning coherently, emotional experience flows without fixation or suppression. When disorganized, experience may oscillate between emotional repression and overindulgence.

Solar Plexus Chakra (Manipura Chakra)

Is associated with transformation, digestion, and identity. It corresponds to the fire element and is located at the navel center. Its traditional color is yellow, symbolizing clarity and transformation, and it is associated with the mahābhūta fire (tejas), with the bīja mantra RAM. This center organizes experiences related to agency, will, self-concept, and the digestion of both food and experience. It governs the digestive organs and is the primary site where Bhavsāgar, the momentum of becoming, is felt. When functioning coherently, there is clarity, appropriate action, and stable self-direction. When disorganized, experience may manifest as control, collapse, anxiety, or compulsive striving.

Heart Chakra (Anahata Chakra)

is associated with connection, relationship, and emotional resonance. It corresponds to the air element and is located at the center of the chest. Its traditional color is green, symbolizing balance and harmony, and it is associated with the mahābhūta air (vāyu), with the bīja mantra YAM. This center organizes experiences related to empathy, connection, compassion, and relational openness. It influences the heart, lungs, and immune system. When functioning coherently, connection is present without attachment or self-loss. When disorganized, experience may appear as emotional withdrawal, codependency, or difficulty with boundaries.

Throat Chakra (Vishuddha Chakra)

Is associated with expression, communication, and clarity. It corresponds to the space element and is located at the throat. Its traditional color is blue, symbolizing openness and clarity, and it is associated with the mahābhūta space (ākāśa), with the bīja mantra HAM. This center organizes experiences related to speech, truth, and the ability to articulate inner experience. It influences the throat, neck, and thyroid system. When functioning coherently, expression is clear, truthful, and appropriate. When disorganized, speech may be suppressed, excessive, or disconnected from inner truth.

Third Eye Chakra (Ajna Chakra)

Is associated with perception, discernment, and meaning-making. It is located between the eyebrows and relates to the functioning of the mind, particularly higher perception and cognition. Unlike the lower chakras, ājñā is not associated with a specific mahābhūta, as it operates beyond elemental organization and marks the transition from elemental experience to mental and perceptual refinement. Its traditional color is indigo, and its bīja mantra is OM or AUM. This center organizes how experience is perceived, interpreted, and understood. It governs insight, pattern recognition, and clarity of perception. When functioning coherently, perception is steady and accurate. When disorganized, experience may be dominated by overthinking, misinterpretation, rigid beliefs, or mental fixation.

Crown Chakra (Sahasrara Chakra)

Represents orientation toward pure awareness and is located at the crown of the head. It lies beyond the mahābhūtas and elemental organization altogether and therefore has no inherent color or form, though it is sometimes symbolized as white or violet light. It has no traditional bīja mantra, as silence is considered its expression. This center reflects the recognition of consciousness itself, beyond identity and form. Sahasrāra does not activate through practice but becomes evident as identification dissolves.

The seven primary chakras are organizing centers within the subtle body that reflect how life experience is structured and expressed through the human system. In addition to these primary centers, there are many smaller energetic junctions throughout the body, including in the palms of the hands, soles of the feet, and along subtle pathways, which contribute to overall energetic functioning. Rather than being something that must be forced open or activated, the chakras naturally organize and harmonize as the flow of prāṇa becomes regulated and coherent. Practices such as mindful awareness, mantra, breath regulation, and meditation support this process by stabilizing attention and refining perception, allowing the chakra system to function in an integrated and balanced way without strain or effort.

Prana Vayus

The prāṇa vāyus are the five primary movement patterns of prāṇa within the body–mind system as described in yoga philosophy. Prāṇa means "life force" or "vitality." Vāyu means "wind" or "movement." Together, the prāṇa vāyus describe how life force moves, not where it lives. These movements govern breathing, digestion, circulation, perception, expression, and integration of experience. Rather than being good or bad, the vāyus are functional directions that must be regulated and coordinated for clarity and balance.

The five vāyus move upward, downward, inward, outward, and pervasively throughout the system.

Prāṇa Vāyu (upward and inward movement)

Prāṇa vāyu governs intake, perception, and mental activity. It is responsible for breathing, sensory awareness, attention, and the movement of energy from the chest toward the head. Its movement is upward and inward.

When prāṇa vāyu is disturbed, the mind may become restless, anxious, scattered, or overly stimulated. When balanced, breath is steady, attention is clear, and perception feels calm and focused.

Practices that support prāṇa vāyu include:
- prāṇāyāma
- gentle backbends
- heart- and chest-opening postures
- slow, mindful breathing

Apāna Vāyu (downward and outward movement)

Apāna vāyu governs elimination, grounding, and release. It is responsible for excretion, menstruation, childbirth, and the ability to let go physically and emotionally. Its movement is downward and outward, from the pelvis toward the earth. When apāna vāyu is disturbed, there may be fear, insecurity, constipation, or difficulty releasing tension. When balanced, there is stability, grounded presence, and a sense of safety in the body.

Practices that support apāna vāyu include:
- grounding postures
- forward folds
- squats
- pelvic floor awareness
- longer exhalations

Samāna Vāyu (inward movement toward the center)

Samāna vāyu governs digestion and integration. Centered at the navel, it gathers prāṇa and apāna and brings them into balance. It is responsible for digestion, metabolism, assimilation of nutrients, and the digestion of experience. When samāna vāyu is disturbed, there may be poor digestion, fatigue, indecision, or difficulty integrating experiences. When balanced, there is steadiness, vitality, and a sense of inner coherence.

Practices that support samāna vāyu include:
• gentle core engagement
• twists
• navel-centered awareness
• steady, rhythmic breathing

Vyāna Vāyu (outward and circulatory movement)

Vyāna vāyu governs circulation and distribution. It moves energy from the center outward to the limbs and throughout the entire body, coordinating movement, circulation, and communication between systems. Vyāna does not initiate action; it distributes whatever state already exists. When disturbed, energy may feel scattered, movement uncoordinated, or the body disconnected. When balanced, the body feels integrated, fluid, and whole.

Practices that support vyāna vāyu include:
• standing postures
• full-body movements
• flowing sequences
• coordinated breath and movement

Udāna Vāyu (upward movement)

Udāna vāyu governs expression, communication, posture, growth, and transition. Its movement is upward, from the chest through the throat and head. Udāna reflects the overall clarity and coherence of the system. When udāna vāyu is disturbed, expression may feel strained, speech rushed, or effort forced. When balanced, there is clarity in communication, ease in posture, and a sense of direction and purpose.

Practices that support udāna vāyu include:
• upright seated postures
• subtle bandha awareness
• chanting or conscious speech
• practices that cultivate vertical lift without strain

Teaching Note (optional but recommended)

The goal of yoga is not to activate the prāṇa vāyus, but to regulate and coordinate them, especially prāṇa and apāna. When the vāyus are balanced, the system stabilizes naturally, allowing deeper stages of observation, liberation, coherence, and līlā (joy) to unfold.

The Three Bandas

The three bandhas, or energetic locks, are subtle techniques used in Haṭha Yoga to contain and direct prāṇa rather than create muscular tension. They are applied primarily in relation to breath, meditation, and prāṇāyāma, and secondarily within āsana.

Root Lock (Mūla Bandha)
Mūla bandha is located at the pelvic floor and involves a subtle lifting and containment at the base of the body rather than a forceful muscular contraction. It supports grounding, stability, and energetic containment by preventing the downward dissipation of apāna vāyu. When applied correctly, mūla bandha supports steadiness, inner support, and energetic integrity, especially during prāṇāyāma and meditation.

Abdominal Lock (Uḍḍīyāna Bandha)
Uḍḍīyāna bandha is centered in the abdominal region and involves a gentle drawing inward and upward of the lower abdomen, traditionally applied on an exhale or breath retention. Rather than simply engaging the core, its function is to draw energy inward toward the center, supporting the unification of prāṇa and apāna through samāna vāyu. When practiced skillfully, uḍḍīyāna bandha supports internal stability, clarity, and containment of attention.

Throat Lock (Jālandhara Bandha)
Jālandhara bandha is applied at the throat by gently lowering the chin while lengthening the back of the neck, without collapsing the chest. Its function is to regulate upward movement, refine the flow of energy toward the head, and stabilize the nervous system. Jālandhara bandha supports clarity, concentration, and containment of upward-moving energy, particularly during prāṇāyāma and seated practices.

Together, the bandhas function as techniques of containment rather than force. They support the regulation and integration of the prāṇa vāyus, helping prevent energetic dispersion and allowing attention to settle naturally. When applied appropriately, the bandhas create the conditions for stillness, clarity, and deeper meditative absorption.

32

33

Koshas

In yoga philosophy, the kośas are layers or sheaths through which human experience is organized, from the most tangible to the most subtle. They are not separate bodies, but interpenetrating dimensions of experience.

Physical Sheath (Annamaya Kośa)

The layer made of food and matter. It includes bones, muscles, organs, tissues, and all physiological systems. It governs structure, nourishment, strength, growth, and decay, and it is the most tangible expression of human existence. This sheath is most directly expressed through vyāna vāyu, which moves outward from the center and circulates through the whole body, distributing vitality through tissues and coordinating movement.

Energy Sheath (Prāṇamaya Kośa)

The vital energy body that animates the physical body. It includes breath, prāṇa, and the subtle movement patterns that regulate vitality and energetic function. This sheath links body and mind and strongly affects stamina, steadiness, and energetic balance. This sheath is primarily governed by the relationship between prāṇa vāyu and apāna vāyu, the two main opposing directional forces, prāṇa moving inward and upward, apāna moving downward and outward, with samāna supporting their balance.

Mental Sheath (Manomaya Kośa)

The mental and emotional layer. It includes thoughts, emotions, memories, desires, sensory impressions, and habitual reactions. This sheath shapes how we interpret life and is where mental fluctuations and emotional reactivity arise. This sheath is strongly shaped by prāṇa vāyu, whose inward and upward movement governs sensory intake, attention, and mental activation, when prāṇa is excessive the mind becomes restless, when regulated the mind settles.

Wisdom Sheath (Vijñānamaya Kośa)

The layer of discernment and clear intelligence. It governs insight, discrimination, conscience, and the ability to observe experience without being absorbed by it. This sheath supports wise choice and the capacity to recognize patterns as patterns. This sheath is supported by udāna vāyu, whose upward and refining movement lifts awareness out of habitual identification and clarifies understanding.

Bliss Sheath (Ānandamaya Kośa)

The subtlest sheath and is associated with deep peace, contentment, and a sense of wholeness. It may be tasted in deep meditation or absorption when the mind is quiet and the system is coherent. This is not pure awareness itself, it is still a sheath and therefore still witnessed. This sheath is reflected when samāna vāyu predominates, drawing energies inward toward the center, equalizing opposing forces, and stabilizing the system into stillness and integration.

When the kośas are transparent, a person is no longer identified with them. They continue to function, but they are no longer mistaken for who we are. Liberation arises through the transparency of the kośas, allowing awareness to recognize itself. This recognition is the ultimate aim of the yoga path.

The Three Gunas

In yoga philosophy, the three guṇas are fundamental qualities of prakṛti, the field of nature from which all forms, experiences, and mental states arise. They govern the behavior of the body, mind, and subtle realms alike. While the doṣas describe physiological patterns within the body, the guṇas describe the qualitative tendencies of perception, thought, emotion, and experience.

Sattva, rajas, and tamas are present in varying proportions in all aspects of existence.

Rajas (Activity, Movement)

Rajas is the quality of activity, motion, and stimulation. It is associated with desire, ambition, striving, and outward engagement with the world. When rajas predominates, the system is driven toward action and achievement, but may also become restless, agitated, or attached to outcomes. Excess rajas can lead to distraction, anxiety, and compulsive activity.

Tamas (Inertia, Obscuration)

Tamas is the quality of inertia, heaviness, and obscuration. It is associated with dullness, resistance, and lack of clarity. When tamas predominates, there may be lethargy, confusion, denial, or stagnation. Excess tamas can manifest as depression, avoidance, ignorance, or unwillingness to change.

Sattva (Clarity, Balance)

Sattva is the quality of clarity, harmony, and balance. It is associated with lightness, calmness, discernment, and inner order. When sattva predominates, the mind is clear, steady, and receptive, supporting insight, ethical action, and inner peace. Sattva creates the conditions necessary for meditation and self-inquiry.

The guṇas are not moral categories, nor are they meant to be eliminated. Yoga practice works to reduce excess rajas and tamas so that sattva can become dominant. However, even sattva remains a quality of prakṛti. Liberation arises not from clinging to sattva, but from recognizing awareness beyond all three guṇas.

The Eight Limbs of Yoga

Even to this modern day and age, yoga in India is often practiced as a way of life, deeply integrated into the culture and daily routines of many Indians. Emphasizing spiritual aspects, philosophical teachings, and holistic well-being. Conversely, yoga in the United States often prioritizes physical fitness and body aesthetics, with some practitioners viewing it primarily as exercise. The spiritual and philosophical dimensions may be less emphasized or integrated differently compared to traditional Indian approaches.

Yoga philosophy encompasses ancient teachings aimed at self-awareness, inner peace, and spiritual growth. Through practices like the Eight Limbs of Yoga, practitioners seek to harmonize the body, mind, and spirit, gaining a deeper understanding of themselves and the universe. Ultimately, yoga is not just about mastering poses; it's about living life with grace and harmony, using these tools to navigate the journey more smoothly.

Always remember that you practice yoga not to get better at doing yoga; you practice yoga to get better at living life.

Limb One: Benevolent Qualities (Yama)

Yama comprises five ethical principles or guidelines for ethical conduct. These principles form the foundation of a yogi's moral and social behavior, helping them cultivate a harmonious relationship with the world around them. Here's a description of each Yama along with real-life practices:

1. Non-Violence (Ahimsa)

Ahimsa emphasizes non-violence in thought, speech, and action towards oneself and others. It involves cultivating compassion, kindness, and empathy.

The sacredness of life lies in recognizing the inherent value and interconnectedness of all living beings. Many spiritual traditions teach that the ultimate purpose of existence is to love and cultivate compassion. Practicing Ahimsa, or non-violence, plays a crucial role in realizing this purpose by fostering a deep sense of love and compassion towards all life forms.

When you practice Ahimsa, you acknowledge the sanctity of life in all its forms. By refraining from causing harm to others—whether through actions, words, or thoughts—you honor the inherent worth and dignity of every being. This practice cultivates empathy, kindness, and respect towards all living creatures, fostering a sense of interconnectedness and unity with the world around you.

Ahimsa enables you to extend love and compassion not only to those you care about but also to strangers, animals, and even the environment. Through acts of kindness, generosity, and forgiveness, you embody the spirit of Ahimsa and contribute to creating a more compassionate and harmonious world.

By practicing Ahimsa, you align yourself with the fundamental purpose of existence: to love unconditionally and to live in harmony with all beings. This practice opens your heart, expands your capacity for empathy, and deepens your connection to the web of life. Ultimately, through the practice of Ahimsa, you realize that love is not just a feeling but a way of being—a guiding principle that leads you toward fulfillment, unity, and the realization of your interconnectedness with all of existence.

Practice Ahimsa by refraining from harming animals or other living beings, practicing patience and understanding in conflicts, and speaking gently to oneself and others even in challenging situations.

2. Truthfulness (Satya)

Satya encourages truthfulness in all aspects of life, including honesty in speech, actions, and intentions. It involves being authentic and sincere in communication.

Embracing Satya, or truthfulness, is vital for finding peace within your mind and setting yourself free. When you commit to living truthfully, you align your thoughts, words, and actions with integrity, bringing clarity and simplicity to your life. Being authentic with yourself and others fosters genuine connections and liberates you from the burden of deception, leading to inner harmony and a sense of freedom. In essence, Satya serves as a powerful tool in the removal of the fluctuations that disturb the peace within the mind, which is the ultimate goal of yoga.

Practice Satya by being truthful in conversations even when it's uncomfortable, representing oneself honestly in interactions, and avoiding spreading rumors or misinformation.

3. Non-Stealing (Asteya)

Asteya, or non-stealing, extends beyond the act of taking physical possessions without permission. It involves respecting others' boundaries, time, energy, and ideas. You recognize the value of integrity, honesty, and respect in your interactions with the world around you. This means not taking advantage of someone's generosity, trust, or goodwill for personal gain.

Asteya also entails acknowledging and appreciating the intellectual property of others. This means refraining from plagiarism, copyright infringement, or unauthorized use of someone else's ideas, creations, or innovations. Instead, you strive to give credit where it's due and seek permission when using or referencing the work of others.

Furthermore, Asteya invites you to cultivate contentment and gratitude for what you have rather than constantly craving more or comparing yourself to others. By embracing a mindset of sufficiency and abundance, you can overcome the urge to steal or hoard resources at the expense of others. One who radiates abundance attracts more abundance into their life. Like chasing butterflies, the moment you become still, the butterflies will chase after you, and you realize that everything you need exists inside of you. Imagine what the world would look like if everyone only took no more than what they actually needed.

Practice Asteya by respecting intellectual property rights, not taking credit for someone else's work, and refraining from stealing time or attention by being punctual and attentive in meetings or conversations.

4. Moderation/Celibacy (Brahmacharya)

Brahmacharya, the principle of moderation, provides a framework for understanding and harnessing sexual energy as the energy of creation. By practicing Brahmacharya, individuals learn to channel this potent force in a balanced and respectful manner, both in their personal lives and creative endeavors. This allows them to harness sexual energy consciously and purposefully, rather than allowing it to govern them unchecked.

When sexual energy is approached with moderation and mindfulness, it becomes a powerful source of creativity and vitality. By directing this energy towards creative pursuits, individuals can infuse their work with passion, innovation, and authenticity.

Moreover, Brahmacharya encourages individuals to cultivate healthy, respectful relationships based on mutual trust, communication, and emotional intimacy. By nurturing meaningful connections, individuals can share and exchange creative energy, fostering collaboration and growth.

In essence, Brahmacharya provides a pathway for individuals to honor the sacredness of sexual energy and its connection to creativity. By practicing moderation and self-discipline, individuals can harness this energy to enrich their lives, relationships, and creative endeavors, ultimately leading to greater fulfillment and harmony.

Practice Brahmachary by balancing work and leisure time, practicing moderation in consumption of food and drink, and maintaining a healthy sense of pleasure in relationships.

5. Non-Grasping (Aparigraha)

Aparigraha teaches acceptance of life's impermanence. However, resisting change and clinging to stability breed fear and anxiety in uncertainty's face. This fear hinders embracing the present fully, leading to suffering.

Grasping often involves comparing oneself to others and coveting what they have. This mindset leads to inadequacy, jealousy, and resentment, stealing inner peace.

"Comparison is the thief of joy" ~ Theodore Roosevelt. Holding tightly to possessions, relationships, or outcomes breeds dissatisfaction, anxiety, jealousy, and constraint. By cultivating non-attachment, individuals discover greater peace, contentment, and freedom in life.

Practice Aparigraha by donating unused belongings to those in need, resisting the urge to accumulate unnecessary possessions, and appreciating experiences and relationships over material wealth.

By practicing the five principles of Yama, individuals can develop greater self-awareness, compassion, and integrity, leading to a more fulfilling and harmonious life both on and off the yoga mat.

Practice Yamas: Each week pick a Yama and apply it to your day to day life through your thought, speech and actions.

Limb Two: Noble Living (Niyama)

Niyama consists of personal observances or ethical guidelines for self-discipline and spiritual development. This limb encompasses practices that cultivate positive qualities and attitudes within oneself. There are five Niyamas:

1. Purity (Saucha): Saucha encompasses various practices aimed at purifying the body, mind, and environment. Physical cleanliness involves regular bathing, grooming, and maintaining personal hygiene. Tidiness extends to keeping living spaces clean and organized, promoting a sense of calm and clarity. Embracing a healthy diet nourishes the body and mind, contributing to overall well-being. Mental purity is fostered through practices such as meditation, mindfulness, and positive thinking, helping to clear away negative thoughts and emotions.

2. Contentment (Santosha): Cultivating contentment involves finding joy and satisfaction in the present moment. Gratitude practices, such as keeping a gratitude journal or expressing thanks daily, help cultivate a sense of appreciation for life's blessings. Mindful consumption encourages contentment with what one has, rather than constantly seeking external validation through material possessions. Acceptance of life's ups and downs with equanimity fosters a deep sense of contentment and peace.

3. Discipline (Tapas): Tapas involves the cultivation of self-discipline and inner strength. Establishing a daily routine helps create structure and consistency in life, fostering discipline and focus. Commitment to regular practice, whether it be yoga, meditation, or exercise, builds resilience and determination. Setting goals and taking disciplined action steps towards achieving them cultivates a sense of purpose and accomplishment.

4. Self-Study (Svadhyaya): Svadhyaya encourages self-reflection and personal growth and introspection. Reading sacred texts, philosophy, or literature that promotes self-awareness provides insights into the nature of the self and the universe. Journaling allows for the exploration of thoughts, emotions, and experiences, deepening self-understanding. Seeking feedback from mentors, peers, or loved ones helps gain perspective and insights into one's strengths and areas for growth.

5. Surrender to the Divine (Ishvara Pranidhana): Ishvara Pranidhana involves surrendering to a higher power or divine consciousness. Prayer, meditation, or contemplation connect individuals with a sense of transcendence and spirituality. Letting go of the need for control and surrendering outcomes fosters trust in the inherent goodness of life. Engaging in acts of service and kindness, without expecting anything in return, reflects a surrender to the divine will and promotes a sense of unity and interconnectedness. That is the deeper meaning of the spiritual greeting "namaste", the light within me honors and recognizes the divine within you.

Practice Niyama: Each week pick a Niyama and put it into practice, For example clean out your closet, read a self-development book, or establish a daily spiritual practice such as yoga, meditation, or pranayama.

Limb Three: Pose (Asana)

Asana refers to the physical postures practiced in yoga. While the primary focus of asana practice is often on the physical body, its benefits extend far beyond mere flexibility or strength. Asana practice promotes physical well-being by improving flexibility, strength, balance, and coordination. Regular practice can help alleviate stiffness, reduce the risk of injury, and enhance overall physical fitness.

Asana practice has profound effects on mental health, helping to reduce stress, anxiety, and depression. The mindful focus on breath and movement fosters a sense of presence and inner peace, calming the mind and improving emotional well-being. This practice also aims to balance the flow of prana (life force energy) in the body, promoting vitality and optimal health. Certain poses stimulate specific energy centers (chakras), helping to remove blockages and restore balance to the body-mind-spirit system.

Asana practice cultivates awareness of the mind-body connection, encouraging practitioners to become more attuned to sensations, emotions, and thoughts arising during practice. This heightened awareness can lead to greater self-understanding and self-acceptance. While often overlooked, asana practice can be a powerful tool for spiritual growth and self-realization. Through the integration of breath, movement, and intention, practitioners can deepen their connection to the inner self and experience moments of transcendence and unity, which is the literal translation of the word "yoga."

Despite its many benefits, asana practice can sometimes become overly focused on aesthetics, such as achieving the "perfect" pose or attaining a certain physical appearance. This emphasis on external appearance can lead to comparison and competition. When practitioners fixate on achieving a particular look or level of performance, they may fall into the trap of comparing themselves to others or engaging in competitive behavior, which can detract from the true purpose of yoga. Pushing the body beyond its limits in pursuit of aesthetic goals can increase the risk of injury. Ignoring the body's signals and forcing oneself into advanced poses without proper preparation or alignment can lead to strain, overuse injuries, or even long-term damage.

Asana practice can sometimes feed the ego, leading practitioners to seek validation or approval from others based on their physical abilities or appearance in certain poses. This can create a false sense of superiority or inferiority and hinder genuine spiritual growth. When the focus shifts solely to achieving a desired aesthetic outcome, practitioners may lose sight of the deeper purpose of yoga, which is to cultivate mindfulness, self-awareness, and inner transformation. This can result in a superficial practice devoid of meaning or depth. One definition of Asana is "to sit quietly within." Many people mistake handstands, inversions, and complicated Asanas as the most important yoga poses. The yogis believe that savasana is the king of all yoga poses, and that is where the yoga actually begins because you are able to drop into a deep meditative state of consciousness. All the other poses practiced in a power yoga class are a means to an end, designed to get you into that transcendental state in savasana.

To avoid getting too caught up in aesthetics, it's important for practitioners to cultivate a balanced approach to asana practice. This involves cultivating mindful awareness, practicing self-compassion, setting clear intentions, and approaching practice with humility and gratitude. By doing so, practitioners can reap the full benefits of yoga while avoiding the pitfalls of excessive focus on aesthetics.

Practice Asana: Even if only for 30 minutes, establish a regular Asana practice three to five times a week and witness the transformation unfold!

Limb Four: Breath Control (Pranayama)

Pranayama is the expansion of life force (prana) through various breath control techniques. In yoga philosophy, the breath is seen as the bridge between the body, mind, and spirit. Pranayama techniques allow practitioners to harness and manipulate the breath, accessing the vital life force energy (prana) that animates all living beings. It promotes physical, mental, and spiritual well-being. Pranayama techniques range from simple breath awareness exercises to more advanced practices involving specific patterns of inhalation, exhalation, and retention.

Pranayama plays a vital role in asana, as it helps synchronize movement with breath, creating a seamless flow of energy throughout the body during yoga postures. By coordinating breath with movement, practitioners can enhance the effectiveness of their asana practice, deepen their stretches, and maintain stability and alignment in poses. It activates the parasympathetic nervous system, inducing a state of relaxation and reducing the physiological effects of stress on the body.

Additionally, pranayama acts as a tool to calm the mind and focus awareness, and serves as a gateway to dropping into deeper states of meditation. Asana practice can sometimes evoke physical sensations, discomfort, or distractions. Through incorporating mindful breathing techniques, practitioners can cultivate a sense of presence and concentration, allowing them to stay centered and grounded amidst the challenges of their Asana practice.

Pranayama practices are integral to the process of awakening the Kundalini energy, leading to spiritual growth, self-realization, and a deeper connection to the divine.

While pranayama offers numerous benefits, it is essential to approach practice with mindfulness, respect for individual limitations, and guidance from a qualified teacher, especially when exploring more advanced techniques. With regular practice and proper guidance, pranayama can become a powerful tool for holistic health and spiritual evolution.

Practice Pranayama: Using ujjayi breath, inhale four counts, exhale four counts. Inhale four counts, exhale five counts. Inhale four counts, exhale six counts. Inhale four counts, exhale seven counts. Inhale four counts, exhale eight counts.

Limb Five: Sense Control (Pratyahara)

Pratyahara is often translated as "withdrawal of the senses." It involves turning the attention inward, away from external distractions, to cultivate a deeper state of self-awareness and inner tranquility.

Pratyahara is a turning point and bridge between the external practices of the previous limbs (asana, pranayama) and the internal practices of meditation and concentration (dharana, dhyana). By withdrawing the senses from external stimuli, practitioners create a conducive environment for meditation and introspection.
In today's fast-paced world filled with constant sensory input, Pratyahara offers a valuable antidote. It allows practitioners to disengage from the external world and find refuge in the inner landscape of the mind. "Knowing others is wisdom, knowing yourself is enlightenment." ~ Lao Tzu, Tao Te Ching

Pratyahara is important because it empowers you to reclaim your inner sovereignty and connect with our true essence.

Shanmukhi mudra, also known as "closing the six gates," is a powerful Pratyahara practice in yoga. It involves using the fingers to gently close the six sensory gates— the eyes, ears, nostrils, and mouth— to withdraw the senses from external stimuli and turn the attention inward. This practice creates a profound sense of inner stillness and tranquility, allowing practitioners to explore the inner landscape of the mind with greater depth and clarity.

By closing the sensory gates, Shanmukhi mudra helps to reduce the influx of sensory input that often overwhelms the mind and distracts us from our internal experience. This withdrawal of the senses creates a sacred space within, where practitioners can cultivate mindfulness, concentration, and self-awareness.

Practice Shanmukhi mudra in a seated or lying position, with the spine tall and the body relaxed. To perform the mudra:
- Sit comfortably with the eyes closed and the hands resting on the knees or thighs.
- Use the thumbs to close the ears.
- Use the index fingers to close the eyes by placing them lightly on the eyelids.
- The middle fingers are placed over the nostrils, gently pressing not fully closing.
- Finally, use the the ring and pink fingers to frame the lips, resting them lightly on the mouth.

With the sensory gates closed, focus on the breath or a chosen point of concentration within the body, such as the heart center or the third eye. Allow the mind to become still and receptive, observing any thoughts, sensations, or emotions that arise without attachment or judgment.

Limb Six: Concentration (Dharana)
Dharana refers to concentration or single-pointed focus. It involves training the mind to remain fixed on a particular object, image, or thought, to the exclusion of all other distractions. Dharana is an essential precursor to meditation (dhyana), as it helps to quiet the fluctuations of the mind and prepare it for deeper states of inner absorption.

In the practice of Dharana, practitioners choose a focal point for their concentration, such as a candle flame, a mantra, the breath, or an image of a deity. The chosen object serves as an anchor for the mind, allowing practitioners to develop heightened levels of focus and attention.

Dharana can be practiced in various ways, including Trataka (Candle Gazing): Focusing the gaze on a candle flame placed at eye level, allowing the eyes to remain steady without blinking. Mantra Meditation: Repetition of a sacred word, phrase, or sound (mantra) to quiet the mind and cultivate a sense of inner peace and stillness. The rhythmic repetition of the mantra helps to anchor the mind and dissolve distractions. Breath Awareness: Bringing attention to the natural rhythm of the breath, observing its flow without trying to control it. This practice helps to center the mind and cultivate present-moment awareness.

Visualization: Imagining a specific image or scene in vivid detail, such as a serene natural setting or a symbol of spiritual significance. Visualization techniques help to engage the mind and deepen concentration.

Dharana strengthens the ability to focus the mind and sustain attention on a chosen object or point of focus, leading to improved concentration and mental clarity. By cultivating single-pointed focus, Dharana promotes mindfulness and present-moment awareness, allowing practitioners to engage more fully with their experiences and activities. Dharana helps to calm the fluctuations of the mind and reduce mental chatter, which is the primary goal of yoga according to Patanjali's Yoga Sutras: "Yoga chitta vritti nirodha."

Practice building concentration in Dharana is similar to building muscle and physical strength, it takes time and dedication. Approach it with a mindset of patience, persistence, and self-compassion, you'll gradually develop greater concentration and inner stability. Just as you wouldn't attempt to lift heavy weights on your first day at the gym, begin with manageable periods of concentration. Start with a few minutes of Dharana practice and gradually increase the duration as you build strength and endurance. If your mind wanders, understand that distractions are natural, and instead of getting frustrated, just as if you would with an innocent child that got distracted and derailed off their path, gently hold their hand and bring them back to focus. Use techniques like repeating a mantra or visualizing the object of concentration to help maintain focus and cultivate mindfulness both on and off the mat to develop greater self-awareness.

Limb Seven: Meditation (Dhyana)

Dhyana is often translated as "meditation" or "contemplation." It refers to the practice of uninterrupted, sustained focus on a single point of meditation. Unlike Dharana, which involves concentration on a specific object or point, Dhyana is characterized by a state of effortless awareness and absorption in the present moment.

In Dhyana, the practitioner enters a state of deep inner stillness and tranquility, where the boundaries between the meditator and the object of meditation begin to dissolve. This state of absorption allows for profound experiences of unity, clarity, and transcendence.

Dhyana unfolds through detachment from any specific outcome or experience, embodying a state of open receptivity and expansion of consciousness. Unlike striving to achieve a particular state of meditation, Dhyana arises naturally when the practitioner relinquishes attachment to results and surrenders to the present moment with acceptance and equanimity.

Moments of Dhyana can feel expansive, as if time has slowed down or even ceased to exist altogether. When immersed in Dhyana, practitioners often experience a sense of timelessness, where minutes feel like moments and hours pass by unnoticed.

Dhyāna is the gateway to samādhi, the final limb of yoga, in which awareness rests in complete absorption and clarity. Through sustained meditation, the mind becomes quiet and receptive to recognizing its true nature.

Practice Dyana after cultivating concentration (Dharana), transition seamlessly into the practice of Dhyana by letting go of effort and control. Rather than actively directing your focus, allow your mind to settle naturally, like a river flowing smoothly without resistance. Release any urge to control your thoughts or experiences and simply surrender to the present moment. By embracing this effortless state of awareness, you'll find yourself seamlessly immersed in the practice of meditation (Dhyana), experiencing deep tranquility and inner stillness.

Limb Eight: Union (Samadhi)
Samadhi represents the culmination of the yogic path. It is not an achievement or altered state created through effort, but a natural condition that becomes evident when identification with mental activity dissolves. In samādhi, awareness is no longer absorbed in thought, memory, emotion, or self-concept. The movements of the mind have settled, and perception rests in clarity.

In this state, the usual sense of separation between the observer, the observed, and the act of observing falls away. What remains is pure awareness, undisturbed and self-luminous. This is often described as union, not because something new is joined, but because the illusion of separation no longer structures experience.
What is traditionally called māyā refers to the veil of misperception created by identification with thought and conditioning. In samādhi, this veil is no longer operative. Awareness recognizes itself directly, without distortion, story, or identity. The world continues to appear, but it is no longer mistaken for the self.

Classical texts describe different degrees of samādhi, ranging from absorbed concentration to complete non-identification. While these stages vary in depth and stability, they share the common quality of transcending ordinary, conditioned consciousness.

Samādhi cannot be forced or manufactured. It arises naturally as the result of sustained regulation, containment, and observation. When the conditions are present and effort relaxes, awareness rests in its own nature.

Samādhi is not an escape from life, but the foundation for living freely. From this clarity, action arises without attachment, fear, or compulsive striving. This is the basis for liberation and the capacity to engage in life as līlā, life lived with ease, presence, and understanding.

Practice Tip: Samādhi is not a technique or a description, it is a state of being recognized. After a physical practice, lie down in Śavāsana and allow the body to fully settle. Let go of all techniques, control, and intention. Rather than trying to experience samādhi, simply notice what remains when nothing is being done. Rest in stillness without seeking or effort. Samādhi is not created through action but recognized when activity subsides. When you are ready to transition out, do so slowly, carrying this quiet clarity into daily life.

Meditation

Meditation is a foundational aspect of yoga, serving as a means to cultivate inner peace, clarity, and self-awareness. At its core, meditation involves training the mind to focus and quiet the incessant chatter of thoughts, emotions, and distractions. It is a practice of turning inward, allowing oneself to become fully present in the moment and to observe the fluctuations of the mind without judgment or attachment.

In the context of yoga, meditation is often viewed as an extension of the physical practice (asana) and breathwork (pranayama), serving to deepen the connection between body, mind, and spirit. Just as the physical postures prepare the body for meditation by releasing tension and creating a sense of ease, breathwork helps to calm the mind and center awareness, laying the groundwork for a successful meditation practice.

The basics of meditation in yoga involve finding a comfortable seated position, closing the eyes, and directing attention inward. This can be done in various ways, from focusing on the breath or repeating a mantra to simply observing the flow of thoughts and sensations without getting caught up in them. The key is to maintain a sense of relaxed alertness, allowing the mind to settle naturally and becoming fully present in the moment.

Meditation can be likened to tending to a garden. Just as a gardener carefully nurtures and tends to their plants, removing weeds and providing nourishment, meditation involves tending to the garden of the mind, cultivating qualities like mindfulness, compassion, and inner peace. With consistent practice, the garden of the mind becomes more vibrant and alive, filled with beauty, tranquility, and flourishing insights.

As one delves deeper into the practice of meditation, they may begin to experience a sense of expansion and interconnectedness, transcending the boundaries of the individual self and tapping into a deeper reservoir of wisdom and intuition. This journey of self-discovery and inner exploration is at the heart of yoga, guiding practitioners towards greater levels of self-realization and spiritual awakening.

In summary, meditation is an essential aspect of yoga practice, offering a pathway to inner peace, self-discovery, and spiritual growth. By incorporating meditation into your daily routine, you can cultivate a deeper sense of presence, awareness, and connection to the true essence of your being.

Styles of Meditation

There are numerous styles and schools of meditation, each with its own unique techniques, traditions, and philosophies. Some of the most well-known styles include:

1. Mindfulness Meditation: Rooted in Buddhist traditions, mindfulness meditation involves paying non-judgmental attention to the present moment, including thoughts, emotions, sensations, and surroundings. This practice cultivates awareness, acceptance, and equanimity.

While in meditation, thoughts will inevitably arise in your mind. Instead of getting caught up in the content of the thoughts or trying to suppress them, simply observe them as they come and go. When you notice a thought arising, mentally label it with a simple word or phrase that describes its content. For example, if you're thinking about what to make for dinner, you might label the thought "planning." If you're worrying about an upcoming deadline, you might label the thought "worrying." After labeling the thought, gently let it go and return your attention to the breath. Imagine the thought drifting away like a cloud passing through the sky of your mind. There's no need to analyze or judge the thought—simply acknowledge it and let it go.

Repeat as needed and continue this process of observing, labeling, and letting go of thoughts as they arise in your mind. You may find that certain thoughts come up repeatedly. That's how you become the observer of your mind patterns and learn how to master your thoughts instead of being a slave to them.

2. Vipassana Meditation: Aside from Buddhist teachings, Vipassana meditation emphasizes insight into the nature of reality through mindfulness of breath and bodily sensations. Practitioners observe the impermanence and interconnection of all phenomena, leading to profound insights and liberation from suffering.

The 10-day Vipassana meditation retreats held in isolated places, such as the desert, offer a unique opportunity for intensive practice and profound transformation. Participants commit to a period of silent contemplation, immersing themselves fully in the practice of Vipassana meditation. Silence is maintained both externally and internally throughout the retreat, creating a conducive environment for deep introspection and self-discovery. Structured schedules, guidance from experienced teachers, and the practice of noble silence support participants as they delve deep into their own consciousness. Set in remote and serene locations, away from the

distractions of everyday life, the intensive nature of these retreats often leads to profound personal transformation. Participants may experience moments of insight, clarity, and liberation as they delve deep into the layers of their own consciousness. The challenges and difficulties encountered during the retreats serve as opportunities for growth and self-discovery.

3. Mantra Meditation: This involves using a mantra—a specific word or phrase—to effortlessly transcend ordinary thought and access deeper levels of consciousness. One definition of the word mantra is "to reinforce the mind." In Sanskrit, the word "mantra" is derived from the roots "man," which means mind, and "tra," which means to protect or be free from.

When you use a silent mantra—a specific word or sound—repeated silently in your mind, it facilitates a state of transcendence. During a mantra meditation session, you sit comfortably with your eyes closed and silently repeat your mantra for about 15-20 minutes.

The mantra "I AM" is the most powerful in the entire universe. Be very mindful of what you casually say after the words "I AM" because whatever you plug in after those two words, whether negative or positive, defines who you become. If you say something like "I am clumsy," "I am the worst," or "I am broke," that is who you become. But if you say something like "I am healthy," "I am wealthy," or "I am at peace," that is also who you become.

"I AM" is often capitalized for emphasis because it represents a powerful affirmation or declaration of one's identity and existence. In spiritual and self-development contexts, "I AM" is seen as a statement of empowerment and self-realization, highlighting the importance of recognizing one's true nature and potential. Capitalizing "I AM" emphasizes its significance and underscores its transformative power in shaping beliefs and perceptions about oneself.

Regular practice of mantra meditation has been associated with a wide range of physical, mental, and emotional benefits, including reduced stress and anxiety, improved focus and concentration, enhanced creativity and problem-solving abilities, and greater overall well-being. Research has also shown that mantra meditation can have positive effects on cardiovascular health, immune function, and overall longevity.

4. Loving-Kindness Meditation (Metta): Metta meditation involves the cultivation of unconditional love, compassion, and goodwill towards oneself and others. You repeat phrases and visualizations to generate feelings of loving-kindness and cultivate a heart-centered awareness.

The word "Metta" is derived from Pali, an ancient language of the Indian subcontinent, and it translates to "loving-kindness." In this practice, you generate and radiate feelings of loving-kindness toward yourself, loved ones, neutral individuals, difficult individuals, and ultimately, all beings.

Sit comfortably in a quiet and relaxed posture and begin by directing loving-kindness towards yourself, silently repeating phrases such as "May I be healthy, may I be happy, may I be at peace". By offering kindness and compassion to yourself, you lay the foundation for extending these feelings to others.

Next, you expand the practice to include loved ones, such as family and friends, by silently repeating similar phrases directed towards them, "May you be healthy, may you be happy, may you be at peace". You then extend loving-kindness to neutral individuals—people you may encounter in daily life but with whom you have no strong emotional connection. This can include acquaintances, strangers, or individuals encountered in passing. You repeat to them, "may you be healthy, may you be happy, may you be at peace"

One of the most challenging and most advanced aspects of Metta meditation is extending loving-kindness towards difficult individuals—those who may have caused harm or difficulty in your life. You cultivate empathy and compassion towards these individuals by recognizing their shared humanity and wishing them happiness and peace. You repeat to them, "may you be healthy, may you be happy, may you be at peace"

Finally, the practice culminates in radiating loving-kindness towards all beings without exception. You visualize your loving-kindness spreading outward like ripples on a pond, encompassing all living beings—humans, animals, and even plants. This expansive feeling of universal love and goodwill fosters a sense of interconnectedness and compassion for all life. You repeat to all beings, "may you be healthy, may you be happy, may you be at peace"

5. Yoga Nidra: Also known as "yogic sleep," Yoga Nidra is a guided meditation practice that induces deep relaxation and conscious awareness of the body, breath, and mind.
Similar to a body scan, you lie down in a comfortable position, such as Savasana (corpse pose), and follow the instructions of a trained guide or teacher. You begin by systematically relaxing your body, sequentially directing your attention to different parts of it.

Yoga Nidra can be a powerful tool for releasing deeply stored trauma in the body. Traumatic experiences, whether physical, emotional, or psychological, can become lodged in the body's tissues and nervous system, leading to chronic tension, stress,

and dysfunction. During Yoga Nidra, you enter a state of consciousness between wakefulness and sleep, where the subconscious mind becomes more accessible. In this state, you can access and explore deeply rooted patterns, beliefs, and emotions that may be contributing to trauma-related symptoms. The systematic relaxation techniques used in Yoga Nidra help calm the sympathetic nervous system, which is responsible for the body's stress response. By inducing a state of deep relaxation, Yoga Nidra allows the body to release tension and deactivate the fight-or-flight response, creating a safe space for processing and healing. By staying present with whatever arises during the practice—whether it's emotions, sensations, or memories— you can gradually release stored trauma and cultivate a greater sense of wholeness and healing.

57

6. Kundalini Meditation: In Kundalini meditation, you'll engage in a blend of ancient yogic techniques called "kriyas." These involve breathwork, chanting, hand gestures or "mudras," and meditation methods—all designed to stimulate and purify your subtle energy system. The repetitive movements, vigorous breathwork, and rhythmic chanting in these practices aim to awaken the dormant Kundalini energy, often described as a coiled snake at the base of your spine, encouraging it to ascend through the shushumna nadi, the central energy line that runs through the spine.

As you dive into Kundalini kriyas, you might feel energy sensations moving along your spine and notice shifts in consciousness and awareness. These practices systematically open and balance your chakras, allowing Kundalini energy to flow freely throughout your subtle body.

Kundalini practices aim to release energetic blockages, heal past traumas, and elevate your consciousness to higher states. It is important to approach Kundalini practices with mindfulness, respect, and guidance from an experienced teacher. Awakening Kundalini energy can be powerful and potentially overwhelming if not approached with care. With proper guidance, you can harness the transformative potential of these practices while ensuring your well-being and safety.

7. Guided Visualization: Guided visualization meditation can be a profound practice for aligning your subconscious mind and energy field with your goals and intentions, particularly when combined with a focus on the chakras, or energy centers, of the body. By moving your awareness through each chakra and imbuing them with the energy of your aspirations, you create a powerful synergy between mind, body, and spirit.

As you journey through each chakra during guided visualization, you'll bring your awareness to specific qualities and attributes associated with each energy center. For example, the root chakra embodies stability and financial security, the sacral chakra represents creativity and passion, and the solar plexus chakra symbolizes personal power and confidence. By envisioning these qualities within yourself and activating them within each chakra, you align your entire being with the energy of your goals.

Through this process, you become a living, breathing conduit for your intentions, embodying the essence of what you wish to manifest in your life. As your subtle body cultivates a deep sense of familiarity with the idea of your goal at the level of the chakras, it begins to permeate every aspect of your being. Your thoughts, words, and actions naturally align with this higher vibration, propelling you forward on the path toward manifestation.

By consistently practicing guided visualization in this way, you create a harmonious resonance between your inner world and outer reality. Your body becomes a vessel for the manifestation of your desires as you energetically attune yourself to the frequency of your goals. This alignment allows you to effortlessly magnetize opportunities, synchronicities, and resources that support the realization of your dreams.

Ultimately, guided visualization meditation offers a potent method for harnessing the creative power of your consciousness and bringing your intentions into tangible manifestation. It is the law of nature that creation happens through thought first, and then it transmutes into physical matter. When you plant a thought seed into your unconscious mind, it lands on the most fertile grounds, and it sprouts to become your reality.

These are just a few examples of the diverse range of meditation styles and schools available. Each style offers a unique approach to cultivating mindfulness, inner peace, self-awareness, and spiritual awakening. It's essential to explore different styles under the guidance of a highly qualified and experienced teacher and find the one that resonates most deeply with your personal preferences, beliefs, and goals.

Bhakti Yoga: Chanting and Kirtan

Bhakti Yoga, often described as the yoga of love, is centered around cultivating a deep and loving relationship with the divine universal intelligence. It emphasizes the expression of pure love, surrender, and devotion toward the divine through various practices and rituals. One of the most prominent practices within Bhakti Yoga is Kirtan.

Kirtan is a devotional practice that involves the communal singing of sacred mantras, hymns, or bhajans in call-and-response style. It is a powerful tool for connecting with the divine and expressing heartfelt devotion. During Kirtan sessions, participants gather together to chant and sing praises to the divine, often accompanied by musical instruments such as drums, harmoniums, and cymbals.

Kirtan serves as a potent means of practicing Bhakti Yoga because it engages the heart, mind, and voice in the expression of devotion. Through the repetition of sacred sounds and melodies, participants immerse themselves in the vibrations of divine love, allowing the music to uplift their spirits and awaken the dormant seeds of devotion within their hearts.

The call-and-response format of Kirtan encourages active participation and creates a sense of unity and connection among the participants. As the chant leader sings a mantra or bhajan, the participants respond by echoing the chant, creating a continuous flow of sound and energy that reverberates throughout the space.

During Kirtan, the rhythmic chanting and singing of sacred mantras produce sound vibrations that resonate not only in the external environment but also within the cells of the body. Sound has a profound effect on the human body, and scientific research has shown that certain frequencies can influence our physiology and mental state.

The sound resonance in the cells of the body during Kirtan has a number of beneficial effects on physical, mental, and emotional well-being. It can help to reduce stress and anxiety, lower blood pressure and heart rate, and promote relaxation and deep states of meditation. The rhythmic chanting also stimulates the release of endorphins and other feel-good hormones, leading to feelings of joy, happiness, and bliss.

Moreover, the sound vibrations generated during Kirtan have a purifying effect on the subtle energy system of the body, the nadis, or energy channels. These vibrations help to clear blockages and imbalances in the energy body, allowing the prana or life force to flow freely throughout the system. This can lead to increased vitality, improved health, and a heightened sense of well-being.

Overall, the sound resonance in the cells of the body during Kirtan creates a profound sense of harmony, alignment, and connection within the individual. It is a powerful tool for healing, transformation, and spiritual awakening, allowing participants to experience the divine presence within and without through the universal language of sound and vibration.

Mantras of Kirtan

AUM

In Yoga, AUM, often written as OM, is a bija (seed) mantra. It is considered to be the primordial sound of the universe, representing the sound of creation during the big bang, or initial existence of consciousness.

The syllable AUM consists of three phonetic components: A, U, and M, each of which represents different aspects of reality:

> A - Represents the waking state of consciousness, the beginning of creation, and the physical realm. It is associated with the aspect of creation, birth, and manifestation.
>
> U - Represents the dream state of consciousness, the intermediary stage between waking and deep sleep. It signifies continuity and transition, as well as the subtle or astral realm.
>
> M - Represents the deep sleep state of consciousness, the state of unconsciousness, and dissolution. It symbolizes the end of creation, death, and the return to the source.

Beyond these three phonetic components, there is a fourth aspect of AUM, often referred to as the silence after the chant. This silence represents Turiya, the state of pure consciousness beyond the waking, dream, and deep sleep states. It signifies the transcendent, formless aspect of reality, beyond words and concepts.

Chanting AUM is considered a powerful spiritual practice, the vibration of the sound resonates throughout the body, aligning the energy centers (chakras) and harmonizing the subtle energy system. AUM is regarded as a sacred and universal symbol of the divine, representing the underlying unity and interconnectedness of all existence.

Gayatri Mantra

The Gayatri Mantra is often recited during morning prayers and meditation practices to invoke divine blessings, wisdom, and spiritual illumination. Many yoga practitioners incorporate the chanting of the Gayatri Mantra into their daily spiritual practice (sadhana).

Om Bhur Bhuvah Swaha
Tat Savitur Varenyam
Bhargo Devasya Dhimahi
Dhiyo Yo Nah Prachodayat

One translation of the Gayatri Mantra is "may the brilliance of the divine essence beyond all realms enlighten us and guide our path."

Lokah Samasta

This Sanskrit mantra translates to "May all beings everywhere be happy and free." It is a powerful invocation of compassion, empathy, and goodwill towards all living beings in the universe. It is usually repeated several times.

Lokah Samasta Sukhino Bhavantu
Lokah Samasta Sukhino Bhavantu
Lokah Samasta Sukhino Bhavantu
Lokah Samasta Sukhino Bhavantu

Ganesha Invocation

The Ganesha Invocation, often recited at the beginning of spiritual practices or endeavors, is a prayer to Lord Ganesha, the Hindu deity revered as "the remover of obstacles" and the patron of arts, sciences, and wisdom. The invocation typically seeks Ganesha's blessings for success, wisdom, and the removal of obstacles. One common invocation to Lord Ganesha is:

Om Gam Ganapataye Namaha

This Sanskrit mantra is a salutation to Lord Ganesha, invoking its divine presence and seeking its blessings for success and the removal of obstacles on one's spiritual or worldly path.

Lakshmi

The mantra "Om Shreem Maha Lakshmiyei Namaha" is a powerful invocation to Goddess Lakshmi, the Hindu deity associated with wealth, prosperity, abundance, and good fortune.

Om Shreem Maha Lakshmiyei Namaha

Chanting this mantra is believed to attract abundance, prosperity, and positive energy into one's life.

65

Pranayama

Pranayama, the fourth limb in Patanjali's Eight Limbs of Yoga, is the expansion and regulation of life force energy, known as "prana." In Sanskrit, "prana" translates to "life force" or "vital energy," and "ayama" means "expansion" or "extension." Therefore, Pranayama can be understood as the intentional expansion and control of this vital energy through breath regulation. Prana is often described as the vital energy that permeates all existence. In many spiritual and philosophical traditions, prana is considered the fundamental life force that sustains all living beings and the universe itself. It is the animating energy that flows through every aspect of creation, from the tiniest cells to the vast cosmos.

In the practice of Pranayama, there are four essential factors that practitioners focus on to regulate and control the breath effectively:

1. Inhalation (Puraka): Puraka refers to the process of inhalation, or breathing in. During Puraka, practitioners take in air slowly and deeply through the nostrils, expanding the lungs and filling them with fresh oxygen. This phase is essential for oxygenating the blood and energizing the body.

2. Retention (Kumbhaka): Kumbhaka is the retention or holding of the breath. After a full inhalation, practitioners may hold the breath for a brief period before exhaling. This phase allows the body to absorb and assimilate the oxygen more efficiently, as well as to regulate the flow of prana within the body.

3. Exhalation (Rechaka): Rechaka is the process of exhalation, or breathing out. During Rechaka, practitioners release the breath slowly and steadily, emptying the lungs completely. This phase removes carbon dioxide and other waste gases from the body, promoting detoxification and relaxation.

4. Empty Space (Shunya): Shunya refers to the empty space or pause that occurs between the exhalation and the next inhalation. This moment of stillness allows practitioners to observe the natural rhythm of the breath and the subtle movements of prana within the body. It is a time for inner reflection and awareness.

By consciously focusing on these four factors—Puraka (Inhalation), Kumbhaka (Retention), Rechaka (Exhalation), and Shunya (Empty Space)—practitioners can deepen their understanding of the breath and harness its power to promote physical, mental, and spiritual well-being through the practice of Pranayama.

When practicing Pranayama, it's important to choose a comfortable and stable posture that creates no effort in the body, so the focus can be solely on the breath. Some of the best positions for practicing Pranayama include:

- Sukhasana (Easy Pose)
- Siddhasana (Accomplished Pose)
- Padmasana (Lotus Pose)
- Ardha Padmasana (Half Lotus Pose)
- Vajrasana (Hero Pose)
- Savasana (Corpse Pose)

Pranayama practices that involve breath retention (Kumbhaka) or forceful breathing techniques are generally contraindicated for pregnant women. These practices can potentially reduce oxygen supply to the fetus and increase the risk of complications during pregnancy. It's essential for pregnant women to consult with a qualified healthcare provider before engaging in any Pranayama practice. However, gentle, mindful breathing techniques like deep diaphragmatic breathing or natural breathing are generally safe and can be beneficial for pregnant women, helping to reduce stress and promote relaxation. Women should also use pranayama gently during their monthly cycle.

Types of Pranayama & Their Sequence

Victorious Breath (Ujjayi breathing) is a Pranayama technique commonly used in yoga practice that involves gently constricting the back of the throat to create a subtle sound resembling ocean waves or the sound of gentle wind. This constriction regulates the flow of air and creates a slight resistance to the breath, resulting in a deep, audible breath.

The technique is typically practiced through both inhalation and exhalation, with the breath moving in and out through the nose. Ujjayi breathing helps to lengthen and control the breath, promoting relaxation, focus, and mindfulness during yoga practice.

Practice Tip:
- Inhale four counts with Ujjayi sound
- Exhale four counts with Ujjayi sound
- Repeat 10 rounds

Even Breath (Sama Vritti) is a Pranayama technique focused on achieving a balanced and steady rhythm of inhalation and exhalation. The aim is to make the duration of the inhalation and exhalation equal in length. Inhaling for a certain count, such as four counts, and exhaling for the same duration, with short retentions in between. This creates a smooth and consistent flow of breath, promoting relaxation and mental clarity.

Practice Tip:
- Inhale for a count of four
- Hold for a count of two
- Exhale for a count of four
- Hold for a count of two
- Repeat ten rounds

Interrupted Inhalation (Viloma 1). The inhalation is divided into segments, with a brief pause or interruptions between. This technique helps to expand lung capacity, increase breath awareness, and promote relaxation.

Practice Tip:
- Inhale using ujjayi for the count of two
- Pause for two counts
- Continue to inhale using ujjayi for another count of two
- Release a long ujjayi exhale for the count of four
- Repeat ten rounds

Interrupted Exhalation (Viloma 2). The ujjayi breath is paused on the exhales.

Practice Tip:
- Inhale using ujjayi for the count of four
- Exhale using ujjayi for the count of tow
- Pause for two counts
- Continue to exhale using ujjayi for another count of two
- Repeat ten rounds

Alternate Nostril Breathing (Nadi Shodhana) is a Pranayama that aims to balance the flow of prana (life force energy) in the body, purify the energy channels (nadis), and harmonize the left and right hemispheres of the brain. It is believed to calm the mind, reduce stress, and promote mental clarity and concentration. During Nadi Shodhana, you use the thumb and ring finger of one hand to alternately close and open the nostrils while breathing. The technique involves inhaling through one nostril, retaining the breath, and then exhaling through the other nostril, followed by a breath retention on the other side before inhaling again. This pattern is repeated, alternating between nostrils.

Nadi Shodhana is often practiced as a preparatory technique for meditation or asana practice, helping to establish a state of balance and inner harmony.

Practice Tip:
- Start by exhaling the breath and empting the lungs
- Seal the right nostril with your right thumb
- Inhale through the left nostril for the count of four
- Seal both nostrils and retain the breath for the count of four
- Seal the left nostril with your left ring finger
- Exhale through the right nostril for the count of eight
- Seal both nostrils and hold for the count of two
- Seal the left nostril with your left ring finger
- Inhale through the right nostril for the count of four
- Seal both nostrils and retain the breath for the count of four
- Seal the right nostril with your right thumb
- Exhale through the left nostril for the count of eight
- Seal both nostrils and hold for the count of two
- Repeat the cycle eight times

Bellows Breath (Bhastrika) is a dynamic breathing technique characterized by forceful inhalations and exhalations through the nose. During Bhastrika, the breath is both rapid and deep, resembling the bellows of a blacksmith. The emphasis is on equal and forceful inhalations and exhalations, generating heat and energy in the body. Bhastrika is often practiced at a moderate to fast pace, with the breath coordinated with vigorous arm movements. It is beneficial for increasing vitality, improving lung capacity, and awakening energy centers (chakras) in the body.

Practice Tip: Start with 1-2 minutes of Bhastrika, gradually increasing to 5-10 minutes as you advance in your practice. Resting 1 minute between each round. If you feel dizzy slow down the intensity and breathe ujjayi

Skull Shining Breath (Kapalabhati) is a more subtle breathing technique focused on rapid and forceful exhalations through the nose, the inhalations will follow passively and naturally. During Kapalabhati, the emphasis is on the forceful contraction of the abdominal muscles to expel air from the lungs. Inhalations occur naturally as a result of the relaxation of the abdominal muscles after each exhalation. Kapalabhati is practiced at a moderate pace, with the exhalations typically being shorter than the inhalations. It is beneficial for cleansing the respiratory system, improving digestion, and increasing mental clarity and focus.

Practice Tip: Start with 1-2 minutes of Kapalabhati, gradually increasing to 5-10 minutes as you advance in your practice. Resting 1 minute between each round. If you feel dizzy slow down the intensity and breathe ujjayi.

Ayurveda

Ayurveda is an ancient system of medicine that originated in India over 5,000 years ago. The word "Ayurveda" is derived from Sanskrit, where "Ayur" means life and "Veda" means knowledge or science. Thus, Ayurveda can be translated as the "science of life" or the "knowledge of life."

Ayurveda approaches the human body holistically, recognizing the intricate interplay between physical, mental, emotional, and spiritual aspects of well-being. It tends to the heart and soul as much as it does to the physical body, acknowledging the importance of balance and harmony in all dimensions of life. In Ayurveda, health is not merely the absence of disease but a state of vibrant vitality and inner balance. Treatments are tailored to address the root cause of imbalances, taking into account an individual's unique constitution (dosha), lifestyle, and environment. Ayurveda employs a wide range of holistic therapies, including diet, lifestyle modifications, herbal remedies, detoxification practices, yoga, and meditation, to restore equilibrium and promote optimal health. In contrast, modern science often views the body as a machine and an all size fits all approach, focusing primarily on diagnosing and treating the symptoms instead of the root cause, with pharmaceutical drugs, surgical interventions, and technological interventions. While modern medicine has made significant advancements in treating acute conditions and emergencies, it may sometimes overlook the deeper, interconnected aspects of health and wellness that Ayurveda seeks to address. Integrating the holistic principles of Ayurveda with the advancements of modern science can offer a more comprehensive approach to healthcare, addressing the needs of the body, mind, and spirit for overall well-being.

Today, Ayurveda continues to be practiced as a traditional system of medicine in India and is gaining popularity worldwide as people seek holistic and natural approaches to health and wellness.

The Three Doshas

In Ayurveda, the three Doshas are fundamental to understanding an individual's constitution, health, and well-being. Each Dosha represents a unique combination of the five elements (ether, air, fire, water, and earth) and governs the body's specific physiological and psychological functions.

Ether and Air (Vata Dosha)

Vata is composed of ether and air elements and is responsible for movement and communication in the body. When in balance, Vata promotes creativity, flexibility, and vitality. However, an imbalance in Vata can lead to symptoms such as dryness, constipation, anxiety, insomnia, and erratic digestion. Physically, Vata imbalance may manifest as cold extremities, weight loss, joint pain, and neurological disorders.

Fire and Water (Pitta Dosha)

Pitta is composed of fire and water elements and governs metabolism, digestion, and transformation in the body. When balanced, Pitta promotes intelligence, courage, and decisiveness. However, an excess of Pitta can lead to symptoms such as acidity, inflammation, anger, irritability, and skin rashes. Physically, Pitta imbalance may manifest as excessive sweating, heartburn, diarrhea, inflammation in the skin, and liver disorders.

Water and Earth (Kapha Dosha)

Kapha is composed of water and earth elements and is responsible for structure, stability, and lubrication in the body. When balanced, Kapha promotes strength, endurance, and nurturing qualities. However, an excess of Kapha can lead to symptoms such as lethargy, weight gain, attachment, congestion, and depression. Physically, Kapha imbalance may manifest as sluggish digestion, excess mucus production, water retention, and respiratory issues such as asthma.

Ayurvedic treatments aim to restore balance to the Doshas through personalized dietary and lifestyle modifications, herbal remedies, detoxification practices, and mind-body therapies. By addressing the root cause of imbalances and promoting harmony among the Doshas, Ayurveda supports the body's innate ability to heal itself and maintain optimal health and vitality.

To harmonize with the heartbeat of the earth involves aligning with natural rhythms and seasonal changes, which impact the balance of Doshas in Ayurveda. Adapting lifestyle, diet, and routines to each season helps maintain equilibrium and fosters a deeper connection with the Earth, promoting balance within ourselves.

PROFESSIONAL ESSENTIALS

PROFESSIONAL ESSENTIALS

Training Methodology

In the journey through Yogi Maha Method, we delve into the heart of teaching—Training Methodology. As we transition into the next chapter, it's crucial to understand why this aspect holds such significance. Training methodology forms the backbone of my teaching philosophy, offering a structured approach to guide both teachers and students along the path of yoga. It's about more than just mechanical instruction; it's about crafting a transcendental experience that empowers and transforms. From artful sequencing and alignment to breathwork and yoga philosophy, each element is carefully woven together to create a holistic framework for teaching and learning. As we explore this next chapter of Training Methodology, we embark on a journey of discovery and growth, uncovering the essence of what it truly means to be a master yoga teacher in Yogi Maha Method.

Yogi Maha Method

As you craft a Yogi Maha Method experience, it's essential to weave together a tapestry of holistic elements that elevate the power yoga class. Remember, you are creating a transcendental experience, not your average yoga class, and you are a Master Yoga Teacher whom people will never forget. The class must have a beginning, middle, and end. These holistic elements, covered below, are what make Yogi Maha Method unique and worldly renowned. These are the secret ingredients that create a transcendental yoga experience and differentiates it from a yoga class that no one remembers. I cannot tell you how many times people line up after class to tell me how profoundly their life was positively changed by my class. "It was like you were talking to me personally." "How did you know what I was going through?" "I needed this so much, especially today." "You saved my life". The truth is I did not know, on an intellectual level, what they were going through. Yoga is a science, and when this ancient science is honored and delivered in the way it was intended to, people cannot help but resonate with it. I am nothing more than an intuitive conduit through which these ancient teachings, taught for thousands of years, flow. Incorporating these holistic elements into your teaching is guaranteed to create the same effect. Be sure to find your voice and unique expression, it is the way that you deliver your instructions that will make people connect to your teachings.

Physical alignment serves as the most critical foundation, ensuring that you incorporate at least five alignment points for each pose. Meditation and pranayama are pillars of the practice, inviting students to explore stillness and breath, nurturing inner peace and tranquility. Sequence the class according to the time of day and season. Early morning classes can be more invigorating to build up energy, while evening classes can be more soothing and relaxing. Incorporate heat-building classes during the winter months and focus on cooling poses and pranayama in the summertime.

Tailor the classes to your students' demographic and skill level. Read the room and adjust your class accordingly, and always honor the class description advertised on the schedule that people signed up for. Students build trust with their teacher when they can feel that the teacher genuinely cares about their experience.

Infuse your class with a profound theme, guiding practitioners on a transformative journey of self-discovery and growth. Ensure to weave the theme throughout the beginning, middle, and end of the class. If the class aligns with a holiday, build a theme around that energy. For example, a gratitude themed class would be perfect for Thanksgiving.

Incorporate the Prana Vayus to honor the subtle energy currents within, awakening vitality and balance. Introduce myths, metaphors, quotes, and stories from yoga philosophy to deepen understanding and connection to the practice.

Explore the depths of the koshas and chakras, unveiling layers of consciousness and self-awareness. Navigate the Gunas, harness the power of Bandhas, and honor the Maha Bhutas to ground students in the essence of creation itself.

In crafting a Yogi Maha Method experience, it is not necessary to incorporate each of these elements. It is important to note that overload can overwhelm both the student and the teacher, weakening the quality of your class, just as not incorporating any of these elements can. A little goes a long way, so aim for quality over quantity. Choose two to three elements carefully and integrate them to guide practitioners on a journey of self-discovery, transformation, and connection to the divine within.

Elements for Consideration:
- Physical Alignment
- Theme of The Class
- Prana Vayus
- Myths Metaphors, Quotes and Stories
- Yoga Philosophy
- Koshas
- Chakras
- Meditation
- Pranayama
- Gunas
- Bandhas and Maha Bhutas

Kramas

In the context of power yoga, "krama" in Sanskrit refers to "stage", a systematic and progressive approach to practicing an asana sequence, where each krama prepares the practitioner for the next.

This is the fundamental Krama for a safe and balanced power yoga sequence. As you advance in your teaching and gain enough knowledge and experience, you can become more creative in the art of sequencing. That is why Advanced Sequencing is a yoga teacher training on its own and is usually delivered as part of a 300 hours Yoga Teacher Training.

Integrative Krama

This is where you set the tone for the class, inviting your students to step away from the noise of their busy lives and shift into a quieter, more centered space within. It's crucial to open strong here, as the first few minutes are paramount in gaining people's trust. Research shows that individuals often form an opinion about the quality of a yoga teacher within the first five minutes of class. Use a warm and calm tone of voice. You can begin with intention setting, cultivating presence and authenticity, and laying the foundation for a transformative experience for your students. This is a great time to introduce yogic breath ujjayi as a foundation for the entire class and introduce any themes. Choose a relaxing pose to begin your integrative series such as child's pose (balasana), easy seat (sukhasana), or even lying down on their backs (savasana) style.

Warm Up Krama

The focus in the Warm-Up Krama is on warming up the major muscles of the body, preparing students for the deeper practice ahead. This is where you can teach Salutations A, Salutations B, along with Warrior Dance. It's the athletic cardio stage (krama) of the class where the body temperature will rise, and students begin to build up a sweat, oxygenating the blood and dissolving mental and emotional tension. Use a tone of voice that motivates students to invigorate their practice and set the stage for a transformative experience, especially in the flow part. You will introduce the alignment points in the setup round. The first side of the setup can be dedicated to alignment, and the opposite side can be dedicated to spiritual guidance. When teaching the flow part, verbal cueing needs to be quick; avoid any wisdom talk here and even alignment points. Only state the breath and name of the pose to keep the pace fast. It's one breath, one movement.

Standing Pose Krama

Standing Pose Krama represents a phase where practitioners delve into more advanced and challenging standing poses. Unlike flowing sequences, this krama emphasizes holding each pose for a longer duration, allowing practitioners to explore their alignment, build strength, and test their balance. Within this krama, you can incorporate poses such as Warrior Two (Virabhadrasana II), Triangle Pose (Trikonasana), Half Moon (Ardha Chandrasana), Reverse Warrior (Viparita Virabhadrasana), Warrior Three (Virabhadrasana III), Hand to Big Toe Pose I (Utthita Hasta Padangusthasana I), Hand to Big Toe Pose III (Utthita Hasta Padangusthasana III). If you are teaching inversions those poses would fit in this Krama. Each of these poses offers unique opportunities for practitioners to deepen their practice and refine their alignment, fostering physical and mental strength, stability, and focus.

Seated Krama

The Seated Krama marks the beginning of the cooling down phase. It offers students a sweet transition following an intense practice, often cherished as a time of deep relaxation and release. During this segment, you can focus on a variety of seated postures, including hip openers, backbends, twists, and forward bends. These poses facilitate the release of tension accumulated during the practice. Use a tone of voice that promotes a sense of calm and ease in both body and mind. Dim the lights and create a soothing environment to enhance relaxation. As students surrender into these soothing postures, they cultivate a deeper connection with their breath and inner selves, allowing for peaceful preparations for the next kramas.

Reclining Krama

In the Reclining Kramas, guide your students to a delicious wind down and prepare for the ultimate relaxation. This is where you can incorporate poses like Happy Baby Pose (Ananda Balasana), Bridge Pose (Setu Bandhasana), supported shoulder stand (Salamba Sarvangasana), and a gentle spinal twist. When executed effectively, this module provides students with a deep and satisfying rest, allowing their bodies to recover from the intensity of the practice. Encourage your students to let go of control in their breath and surrender into each pose, creating a sense of ease and rejuvenation as you guide them to drop into a deeply meditative savasana.

Closing Ritual

Conclude the class with a powerful ending. When bringing your students out of Savasana, do so gently, guiding them to come up to an easy seated position. If you introduced a theme, ensure to bring it full circle for a complete experience. You can guide them to chant "Om" and bring the hands together in Anjali mudra, the prayer position, then allow for several moments of silent contemplation. Encourage them to carry the equanimous energy they cultivated during the practice into the rest of their day, reminding them that real yoga practice extends beyond the mat and into their everyday lives.

Krama Sequences

Integrative Krama

Starting Position: Child's Pose / Balasana. Establish ujjayi breathing. Take a few moments to center yourself and connect with your breath.

Transition: Rise to all fours.

Inhale: Cow/Bitilasana.

Exhale: Cat/Marjaryasana: repeat Cat and Cow five times.

Transition: Return to all fours.

Inhale : Lift the right leg up for Sun Bird

Exhale: Lift the left arm up for Sun Bird

Inhale: Lift the left leg up for Sun Bird

Exhale: Lift the right arm up for Sun Bird

Inhale: Plank Pose: hold for five breaths.

Exhale: Four Limb Staff Pose/Chaturanga Dandasana.

Inhale: Cobra/Bhujangasana: five times.

Exhale: Downward Facing Dog/Adho Mukha Svanasana: hold for five to ten breaths.

Inhale: Bend the knees and look between the hands

Exhale: Step to the top of the mat, arriving in Standing Forward Fold/Uttanasana.

Inhale: Half Forward Fold/ Ardha Uttanasana.

Exhale: Standing Forward Fold/Uttanasana.

Inhale: Mountain Pose/ Tadasana.

Notes:

This sequence is designed to introduce ujjayi breath and integrate it with movement, promoting strength, flexibility, and mindfulness.

Sun Salutation A / Surya Namaskar A - Warm Up Krama

Starting Position: Mountain Pose / Tadasana with hands in prayer (Anjali Mudra)

Inhale: Upward Salute/Urdhva Hastasana.
Exhale: Standing Forward Fold/Uttanasana.
Inhale: Half Forward Fold/ Ardha Uttanasana.
Exhale: Step to Plank Pose or jump to Four Limb Staff Pose/ Chaturanga Dandasana.
Inhale: Cobra/Bhujangasana or Upward Facing Dog/Urdhva Mukha Svanasana.
Exhale: Downward Facing Dog/Adho Mukha Svanasana: hold for five breaths.
Inhale: Bend the knees and look between the hands
Exhale: Step to the top of the mat, arriving in Standing For-ward Fold/Uttanasana.
Inhale: Half Forward Fold/ Ardha Uttanasana.
Exhale: Standing Forward Fold/Uttanasana.
Inhale: Upward Salute/Urdhva Hastasana.
Exhale: Bring the hands to prayer (Anjali Mudra)
Repeat the series five times.

Notes:
Ensure smooth transitions between poses, maintaining steady and mindful breathing. Focus on alignment and fluidity in each posture. Modify poses as needed to suit your practice level. This sequence is designed to warm up the body, integrating breath with movement and preparing for a deeper yoga practice.

Sun Salutation B / Surya Namaskar B - Warm Up Krama

Starting Position: Mountain Pose / Tadasana with hands in prayer (Anjali Mudra)

Inhale: Chair Pose/ Utkatasana.
Exhale: Standing Forward Fold/Uttanasana.
Inhale: Half Forward Fold/ Ardha Uttanasana.
Exhale: Step to Plank Pose or jump to Four Limb Staff Pose/ Chaturanga Dandasana.
Inhale: Cobra/Bhujangasana or Upward Facing Dog/Urdhva Mukha Svanasana.
Exhale: Downward Facing Dog/Adho Mukha Svanasana.
Inhale: Lift the right leg up
Exhale: Step the right foot between the hands and spin the back foot flat
Inhale: Warrior I/Virabha-drasana I.
Exhale: Step to Plank Pose and lower to Four Limb Staff Pose/Chaturanga Dandasana.
Inhale: Cobra/Bhujangasana or Upward Facing Dog/Urdhva Mukha Svanasana.
Exhale: Downward Facing Dog/Adho Mukha Svanasana.
Inhale: Lift the left leg up
Exhale: Step the left foot between the hands and spin the back foot flat
Inhale: Warrior I/Virabha-drasana I.
Exhale: Step to Plank Pose and lower to Four Limb Staff Pose/Chaturanga Dandasana.
Inhale: Cobra/Bhujangasana or Upward Facing Dog/Urdhva Mukha Svanasana.
Exhale: Downward Facing Dog/Adho Mukha Svanasana.
Inhale: Bend the knees and look between the hands
Exhale: Step to the top of the mat, arriving in Standing For-ward Fold/Uttanasana.
Inhale: Half Forward Fold/ Ardha Uttanasana.
Exhale: Standing Forward Fold/Uttanasana.
Inhale: Upward Salute / Urdhva Hastasana

Repeat the series four times, one on each side. Hold each pose for five breaths in the first round (the set up round). Flow the following three rounds, linking one breath to one movement.

Notes:
This stage ignites the internal element "Maha Bhuta" fire, known as "Agni", by seamlessly synchronizing movement and breath. As the body flows through dynamic sequences, heat builds up, warming the muscles and increasing circulation. This warmth enhances flexibility, facilitating deeper stretches and a broader range of motion.

Warrior Dance - Warm-Up Krama

Transition: Once Sun Salutations B are complete, there is a one-time transition to warrior dance. From Mountain Pose/Tadasana with hands in prayer (Anjali Mudra).

Inhale: Upward Salute/Urdhva Hastasana.

Exhale: Standing Forward Fold/Uttanasana.

Inhale: Half Forward Fold/ Ardha Uttanasana.

Exhale: Step to Plank Pose or jump to Four Limb Staff Pose/ Chaturanga Dandasana.

Inhale: Cobra/Bhujangasana or Upward Facing Dog/Urdhva Mukha Svanasana.

Exhale: Downward Facing Dog/Adho Mukha Svanasana.

Warrior Dance Begins Here

From Downward Facing Dog/Adho Mukha Svanasana.

Inhale: Lift the right leg up.

Exhale: Step the right foot between the hands and spin the back foot flat

Inhale: Warrior I/Virabha-drasana I.

Exhale: Warrior II/Virabha-drasana II.

Inhale: Reverse Warrior/ Viparita Virabhadrasana.

Exhale: Extended Side Angle Pose/ Parsvakonasana.

Inhale: Reverse Warrior/ Viparita Virabhadrasana.

Exhale: Step to Plank Pose and lower to Four Limb Staff Pose/Chaturanga Dandasana.

Inhale: Cobra/Bhujangasana or Upward Facing Dog/Urdhva Mukha Svanasana.

Exhale: Downward Facing Dog/Adho Mukha Svanasana.

Repeat on the left side. Repeat the series four times, one on each side. Hold each pose for five breaths in the first round (the set up round). Flow the following three rounds, linking one breath to one movement.

Notes:

In this stage, the essence of "vinyasa" comes alive as each movement flows seamlessly with the breath. Synchronizing breath and movement improves cardiovascular health, increases heart rate, and lays the foundation for mastering advanced balancing poses in the practice ahead.

Standing External - Standing Krama

Downward Facing Dog/Adho Mukha Svanasana.

Inhale: Lift the right leg.

Exhale: Step the right foot between the hands and spin the back foot flat

Inhale: Warrior I/Virabha-drasana I.

Exhale: Warrior II/Virabha-drasana II.

Inhale: Triangle Pose/Trikonasana: hold for five breaths.

Exhale: Half Moon Pose/ Ardha Chandrasana: hold for five breaths.

Inhale: Transition smoothly.

Exhale: Warrior II/Virabha-drasana II.

Inhale: Reverse Warrior/ Viparita Virabhadrasana.

Exhale: Step to Plank Pose and lower to Four Limb Staff Pose/Chaturanga Dandasana.

Inhale: Cobra/Bhujangasana or Upward Facing Dog/Urdhva Mukha Svanasana.

Exhale: Downward Facing Dog/Adho Mukha Svanasana.

Repeat on the left side. This module has only one complete cycle.

Notes:

The external standing sequence emphasizes stability, strength, and alignment through standing postures. Major muscle groups like the legs and core are engaged for a substantial portion of this stage, which builds strength and endurance while improving balance and proprioception.

Standing Balancing - Standing Krama

Downward Facing Dog/Adho Mukha Svanasana.

Inhale: Lift the right leg.

Exhale: Step the right foot between the hands.

Inhale: Crescent Pose: hold five breaths.

Exhale: Bring the hands to prayer Anjali Mudra

Inhale: Lean forward

Exhale: Transition to Warrior III/Virabha-drasana III: hold for five breaths.

Inhale: Come to stand bringing the left knee to the chest.

Exhale: Transition to Hand to Big Toe Pose I / Utthita Hasta Padangusthasana I.

Inhale. Transition to Hand to Big Toe Pose II / Utthita Hasta Padangusthasana II.

Exhale: Return to Hand to Big Toe Pose I / Utthita Hasta Padangusthasana I.

Inhale: Switch the grip of your hands

Exhale: Transition to Hand to Big Toe Pose III / Utthita Hasta Padangusthasana III.

Inhale: Gaze to the front of the mat

Exhale: Return to Mountain Pose/Tadasana with hands in prayer (Anjali Mudra).

Inhale: Move to Chair Pose/ Utkatasana.

Exhale: Twisting Chair Pose/ Parivrtta Utkatasana facing the left: hold for five breaths.

Inhale: Return to Chair Pose/ Utkatasana.

Exhale: Mountain Pose/Tadasana with hands in prayer (Anjali Mudra).

Inhale: Upward Salute / Urdhva Hastasana

Exhale: Standing Forward Fold/Uttanasana.

Inhale: Half Forward Fold/ Ardha Uttanasana.

Exhale: Step to Plank Pose or jump to Four Limb Staff Pose/ Chaturanga Dandasana.

Inhale: Cobra/Bhujangasana or Upward Facing Dog/Urdhva Mukha Svanasana.

Exhale: Downward Facing Dog/Adho Mukha Svanasana.

Repeat on the left side. This module has only one complete cycle.

Notes:

Ensure smooth transitions between poses, maintaining steady and mindful breathing. Modify poses as needed to suit your practice level.

Seated Krama

Downward Facing Dog/Adho Mukha Svanasana: hold for five breaths.
Hero's Pose/Virasana or Reclining Hero's Pose/ Supta Virasana: hold for five breaths.
Camel Pose/Ustrasana: hold for five breaths.
Bound Angle Pose/Baddha Konasana: hold for five breaths.
Seated Forward Fold/Paschi-mottanasana: hold for five breaths.

Notes:
This seated sequence focuses on deep stretching and opening of the hips, thighs, and spine, promoting flexibility and mobility in the lower body. Exploring the sensation and finding ease within the stretch allows time for the body to begin the cooling down phase.

Reclining Krama

Transition: Recline onto the back and come to Knees to Chest/Apanasana: hold for five breaths.
Happy Baby Pose/Ananda Balasana: hold for five breaths.
Reclining Pigeon/Thread the Needle: hold for five breaths on each side.
Bridge Pose/Setu Bandha Sarvangasana or Upward Facing Bow Pose/Urdhva Dhanurasana: hold for five breaths.
Plow Pose/Halasana: hold for five breaths.
Shoulder Stand/Sarvan-gasana: hold for five breaths.
Shoulderstand Exit | Karnapidasana: hold for five breaths.
Fish Pose/Matsyasana: hold for five breaths.
Knees to Chest Pose/Apan-asana: hold for a couple of breaths.
Spinal Twist both on the right and left side.
Corpse Pose/Savasana: hold for several minutes.

Notes:
This reclining sequence focuses on releasing tension and promoting relaxation in the body and mind. Each pose is held for five breaths or as specified, allowing for a gradual transition towards a deeply meditative savasana. Knees to Chest/Apanasana is the hub pose for this krama and can be added in the transition between posees.

Closing Ritual

Transition: Come up to an easy seated position.
Hand Gesture (Mudra): Bring the hands to Anjali Mudra (prayer position) at the heart center.
Chanting: Chant OM three times, allowing the sound to resonate deeply within, connecting body, mind, and spirit.

Notes:
This closing ritual invites a moment of stillness and reflection, grounding the practice and honoring the journey taken on the mat. Anjali Mudra symbolizes unity, which is the translation of the word "Yoga," acknowledging the divine within and around us. Chanting OM three times creates a sacred vibration, fostering a sense of resonance that concludes the practice. Allow a moment to bask in the serenity of this closing ritual, feeling the calmness and centeredness it brings within.

Pace

Yogi Maha Method is a power yoga style also known as vinyasa yoga. It is a dynamic and flowing style of yoga where movement is synchronized with breath. Sequences of yoga poses are linked together in a continuous flow, creating a smooth and fluid transition from one pose to another. The word "vinyasa" itself means "to place in a special way" or "to arrange in a certain manner," emphasizing the intentional sequencing of poses. This style of yoga often incorporates sun salutations, standing poses, balancing poses, inversions, seated and reclining poses, providing a balanced practice that builds strength, flexibility, stamina, balance and mindfulness.

It is important to note that each class must have an arc—a beginning, middle, and end. Start the class gently, warming up the body, then gradually intensify the movement before cooling down and arriving into stillness in Savasana.

In a power yoga class, students sign up expecting an invigorating practice. They enjoy being challenged physically and mentally. Incorporating at least one or two new advanced yoga poses that the class slowly builds up will keep the students engaged, a practice known as building to a peak pose. The class can include one peak pose or multiple peak poses. Having a breakthrough in a yoga pose is an exciting experience for students. Students become bored if the teacher teaches the same yoga poses repeatedly, and they anticipate what to expect and what the teacher will say before it is said. Therefore, it is important for the teacher to prepare for each class and keep their students guessing and both physically and mentally stimulated.

When the yoga teacher is consistent with their overall teaching style, it builds trust between the teacher and the student. The students know what experience to expect (not what poses to expect) when they sign up for the class. Although you can adapt to the time of day, season, and demographic in the room, it is important not to completely change the teaching style, and the class description on the schedule. For example, making the class too easy may turn it into a gentle yoga class rather than a power yoga class. This may leave students feeling disappointed, as it's not what they signed up for.

94

Environment

When the yoga teacher creates a nurturing environment, it sets the tone for a transformational experience. People come to yoga seeking a sacred haven away from the noise of the outside world. Smudging the room and engaging the sense of smell immediately facilitate a mental shift. Adjusting the lighting to create a soothing environment for the eyes also helps.

While traditionally, music is not played in yoga classes, in our modern age, people enjoy a curated playlist that aligns with the class's pace. For instance, at the beginning, softer music sets a serene atmosphere, gradually transitioning to more energizing tunes during the flow to motivate and focus the students. As the class cools down towards the end, the music slows down, fostering relaxation and mindfulness. During Savasana, binaural beats or theta frequencies are recommended to enhance the relaxation experience. It's crucial to choose music that is soothing, positive, and uplifting, as students can enter a transcendental state of mind, unlocking the subconscious.

The primary goal of the yoga teacher is to elevate the frequency in the room and foster an uplifting environment, refraining from discussing politics or negative events, whether personal or cultural. There's already enough of that outside the yoga room, and people come to class to seek refuge from that energy. Visualizing as a teacher that all personal problems are left behind the door of the yoga room helps dedicate this time solely to the health and well-being of the students.

Cueing

Verbal

What makes Yogi Maha Method uniquely successful than most yoga teacher trainings out there, is its emphasis on teaching the majority of the class through verbal cues. In the previous chapter, we discussed the benefits of this style for the students: it protects the safety of their neck, enables deeper meditative states by focusing energy inward, and strengthens the neurological connection between mind and body. From the teacher's perspective, it also minimizes wear and tear on the body. Teaching several times a week, or even daily, can lead to muscle atrophy and is not a sustainable means of livelihood. Injuries or pregnancy can further complicate matters for teachers who rely heavily on physical demonstration. I've witnessed many yoga instructors lose their primary source of income due to this reliance. Verbal cueing not only respects the teacher's body but also allows for greater presence in the class. Teachers can move around the room, provide hands-on adjustments or verbal modifications, and inspire students with a calming tone of voice. Conversely, when teachers participate in the class alongside students, they may become breathless and find it challenging to maintain a steady tone.

Visual

If students in the classroom struggle to follow the teacher's verbal cues, visual demonstration can be provided. The teacher should stand in front of the class if they're facing forward, or go to the side the students are facing and align themselves facing them. It's essential for the teacher to maintain a heart-to-heart connection, avoiding turning their back to the students for energetic reasons. Mirroring is crucial, ensuring the right side of the teacher corresponds to the left side of the students, which aids in maintaining clarity and connection. Another effective visual technique involves standing next to a student who demonstrates the pose correctly, as students typically follow the teacher with their gaze. By positioning close to the student and indicating their alignment, the teacher can effectively use them as a pose demonstrator.

Physical
Physical adjustments should only be used as a last resort, with extreme caution exercised by the yoga teacher. It's essential to be mindful that the student may have an injury hindering proper pose alignment. Prioritize verbal cues first, followed by a visual demonstration, before resorting to physical adjustments. When making physical adjustments, gentle pressure should be applied to avoid causing injury or discomfort. It is important to first stabilize yourself and your student. Make adjustments in sync with the rhythm of the student's breath. Offer assistance with props and provide guidance on how to use them effectively. Additionally, the teacher should be conscious of where they place their hands on the student's body and intuitively assess whether physical contact is appropriate. Some teachers prefer to ask for permission before making hands-on adjustments at the beginning of class, respecting students' privacy and comfort levels.

Class Management

Effective class management ensures that students have a fulfilling and rewarding yoga experience while fostering a sense of community and connection within the class.

Arriving 15 minutes before class begins allows the yoga teacher to adequately prepare the space and themselves. The energy of yoga starts with the teacher, so being punctual sets a calm tone for the students. Arriving early provides time to set up the space, sage the room, adjust lighting, and connect the music. It also allows for greeting students, answering questions, and creating a welcoming atmosphere. Additionally, this extra time enables the teacher to center themselves and mentally prepare for the class.

Creating an inclusive environment where students of all levels, backgrounds, and body types feel welcome and supported is essential. Addressing any challenges or disruptions in the class calmly and effectively while maintaining focus and positivity ensures a smooth experience for everyone. Ending the class on time with a period of relaxation or meditation allows students to integrate their practice and leave feeling refreshed and balanced. Making eye contact and saying goodbye to the students as they leave creates a personal connection and fosters a sense of community. This attention to detail is what creates an unforgettable experience and keeps students coming back for more.

Professional Development

Professional development in yoga involves ongoing learning and growth to enhance teaching skills, deepen knowledge of yoga philosophy and anatomy, and stay updated on industry trends and best practices. This can include attending workshops, trainings, and conferences, pursuing advanced certifications, reading books, engaging in self-study and research, and seeking mentorship from experienced teachers. It also involves maintaining a regular personal practice to continue embodying the principles of yoga and evolving as a practitioner and teacher. Professional development in yoga is crucial for providing high-quality instruction, supporting student needs, and fostering personal and professional fulfillment in the yoga community.

Professionalism

Yoga teachers are held to high standards, embodying the principles of the Niyamas in the Eight Limbs of Yoga. They are viewed as leaders in their community, as they inspire and guide others. Therefore, establishing healthy boundaries with students is vital. While students may seek friendship or even more, maintaining a professional relationship upholds the integrity of the student-teacher dynamic. Similar to the relationship one has with a therapist, where maintaining professional boundaries is essential for the efficacy of the practice. Crossing this line may lead students to seek guidance elsewhere, as it can compromise the trust and respect within the student-teacher relationship.

Cleanliness

Maintaining cleanliness, both in appearance and in the yoga room, aligns with the principle of Saucha, a part of the Yamas in the Eight Limbs of Yoga. Saucha emphasizes purity and cleanliness, both externally and internally. By upholding this principle, a yoga teacher fosters an environment conducive to physical, mental, and spiritual well-being. This involves dressing neatly and appropriately and ensuring that shoes are left outside the yoga room to prevent bringing in dirt or impurities. Cleanliness in appearance demonstrates respect for oneself and others. A clean yoga room promotes serenity and focus during practice. Properly aligned and synchronized yoga mats contribute to the harmonious flow of energy within the space, enhancing the overall experience for students.

Yoga Alliance

Yoga Alliance is a global organization that sets standards for yoga teacher training and registers qualified teachers. It offers resources like continuing education courses and networking opportunities.

In Yoga Alliance, a Registered Yoga Teacher (RYT) is an individual who has completed a yoga teacher training program that meets Yoga Alliance standards and has been registered with the organization. While registration is not required, it can provide credibility and recognition within the yoga community.

Continued Learning

One of the laws of nature is that "if you are not growing, you are dying." The interpretation of this principle is that stagnation can lead to decline. Becoming a master yoga instructor hinges on continued learning. A master instructor consistently expands their knowledge, and as they evolve, so do their students. Yoga is a vast and multifaceted discipline, encompassing physical postures, breathwork, meditation, philosophy, and more. By engaging in ongoing education, teachers can expand their understanding of these aspects, enhance their teaching methods, and offer greater value to their students.

The Business of Being a Yogi

"Success is liking yourself, liking what you do, and liking how you do it." - Maya Angelou. Being a professional yoga teacher also means being a small business owner or entrepreneur. You can be both spiritual and successful in business. Leading a business differs from being an employee; there's no supervisor providing directives. Therefore, it's crucial for a yoga teacher to forge their own path, starting from within. Understanding their strengths and teaching style and finding their authentic voice are paramount. This is why self-study (svadhyaya) in Limb two of the Eight Limbs of Yoga is often emphasized in many other ancient wisdom traditions.

Find Your Voice

Yoga teachers can find their dominating archetype to harness their teaching style by reflecting on their strengths, passions, and values. Archetypes include:

Leader: A yoga teacher who naturally takes charge, inspires others, and leads by example. They thrive in guiding students through their practice, setting the tone for the class, and providing clear direction.

Connector: A yoga teacher who excels in building relationships, fostering community, and creating a sense of belonging. They thrive in connecting with students on a personal level, cultivating a supportive environment, and facilitating meaningful connections among practitioners.

Expert: A yoga teacher who is highly knowledgeable, skilled, and experienced in yoga philosophy, anatomy, and teaching methodologies. They thrive in sharing their expertise, guiding students with precision and clarity, and continually expanding their knowledge base.

Mentor: A yoga teacher who serves as a trusted advisor, guide, and role model for students on their yoga journey. They thrive in offering personalized guidance, support, and encouragement, helping students navigate challenges, and empowering them to reach their full potential.

Ultimately, yoga teachers may resonate with one or more of these archetypes based on their unique combination of skills, interests, and aspirations. By identifying their primary archetype(s), they can align their teaching approach and style to better serve their students and fulfill their own purpose as instructors.

103

Find Your Happy Place

You attract who you are. Discovering your unique teaching style involves exploring various experiences that you naturally gravitate towards such as spiritual, scientific, mystical, mythological, astrological, and storytelling approaches. Be honest with yourself because if you do what you love you never work a day in your life. Ask yourself a series of questions to uncover your preferences:

- Do you enjoy teaching private sessions?
- Are you inclined towards corporate settings?
- Do you thrive in studio environments?
- Are retreats more aligned with your teaching style?
- Do you prefer teaching at big events?
- Are you open to collaboration with other instructors?
- Do you find satisfaction in subbing for other teachers?
- Are you passionate about teaching kids?
- Do you feel drawn to teaching specific demographics, such as women, men, LGBTQ+, or non-binary individuals?
- Are you interested in teaching sobriety-focused classes?
- Do you want to incorporate trauma-informed practices into your teaching?
- Are you passionate about teaching athletes?
- Do you enjoy infusing entertainment into your classes?
- Are you interested in teaching in the medical field?
- Do you have a desire to travel and teach in various locations?

Find Your Community

Discover your niche and tailor your marketing efforts to target the smallest viable audience. Remember, less is more! While demographic factors like age, gender, income, and marital status are crucial, consider delving deeper into their interests and lifestyle choices. Explore where they shop, their dietary preferences, reading and viewing habits, and the influencers they follow. Understand their spiritual, corporate, creative, or conservative inclinations. Identify the events that capture their interest and align with their values. This holistic understanding allows for more targeted and effective marketing strategies.

Marketing

Marketing as a yoga teacher involves showcasing your unique offerings, connecting with potential students, and building a thriving community. In the next few pages I will cover some key strategies.

Master the Message

Once you've defined your identity and connected with your community, focus on mastering your message delivery. Remember, a confused client is a lost client. Keep it concise and clear across all platforms. Your elevator pitch should address:

1. Who you are: Your identity as a yoga teacher
2. What you do: The services you offer and how you deliver them
3. The problem you solve: The specific needs or challenges you address for your clients
4. How you're different: What sets you apart from other yoga teachers
5. Who your work serves: The audience or community you aim to support and uplift

For example:
- "I help seekers of transformation tap into their innate powers of creation through my yoga classes and techniques so they can manifest their best life"
- "I help people looking to change careers find their calling through my yoga teacher training. So they can finally feel fulfilled and love their work"
- "I help women who are stuck in unfulfilling relationships and want to feel loved to activate their ability to attract the love that they deserve through tantra yoga"

Find Your Own Mission Statement
I help_____(type of person). WHO are struggling with _____problem. AND want to_____result + feeling.

OR

I/_____(what you do) FOR _____type of person WHO want to _____result + feeling.

Finding your mission statement requires time (sometimes years to develop), experience, and trial and error. Be compassionate with yourself and trust that you will find your way.

Your Public Presence

Your public presence as a yoga teacher is more than just marketing—it's about building a genuine community rooted in trust and loyalty. As the leader of this community, you have a responsibility to uphold high ethical standards and lead by example. Here are some key elements to consider when establishing your public presence:

- Create a professional and authentic website that exudes your unique offering
- Develop a logo, color theme, and tagline that reflect your brand identity
- Craft a mission statement that communicates your values and purpose
- Invest in professional photos that capture your essence and professionalism
- Offer free online content, such as classes or workshops, to engage with your audience and showcase your expertise
- Collect emails to stay connected with your community and share newsletters
- Consistently host free group classes online to build rapport and maintain visibility
- Utilize platforms like Instagram, Insight Timer, YouTube, TikTok, and SoundCloud to reach a wider audience and share your teachings
- Promote your events through email newsletters, social media posts, and collaborations with business partners.
- Make your posts authentic and genuine, using your own voice and incorporating relevant hashtags.
- Ensure your online presence is cohesive across platforms, including your website, social media profiles, business cards, and email signature.
- Maintain an updated bio highlighting your qualifications, certifications, and continued education endeavors.

By prioritizing authenticity, consistency, and community-building, you can establish a strong public presence as a yoga teacher that resonates with your audience and fosters long-term connections.

Corporate

In a corporate yoga setting, it's essential to tailor your teaching approach to meet the needs and preferences of busy professionals. Avoiding spiritual themes, Sanskrit, or ancient terminology and focusing on practical benefits is key. Keep the content simple and straightforward, ensuring it resonates with diverse beliefs and backgrounds. Prioritize topics such as neuroscience insights, stress management techniques, quality of sleep, productivity tips, and enhancing focus and concentration. Additionally, explore ways to foster inspiration, creativity, resilience, teamwork, compassion, loving-kindness, self-confidence, and time efficiency. Provide short and simple tools that employees can easily integrate into their hectic schedules. Make the class at all levels focus on de-stressing the body and the mind, empowering them to enhance their well-being and performance in the workplace.

Privates

For yoga teachers looking to offer private sessions, having certain tools and practices in place can enhance the experience for both you and your clients. Start by establishing clear client guidelines and obtaining necessary health information through a client health sheet. Keep a detailed class log sheet to track progress and sessions. Ensure protection for yourself and your clients with a release of liability form and liability insurance. Exchange referrals with other professionals to expand your client base. Promote your availability through various channels and offer gift certificates for special occasions. Consider different locations for sessions, such as your home, outdoors, or rented spaces, and maintain consistency in your offerings. Regularly check in with your clients to address any concerns or adjustments needed. Provide additional support as needed and remember important dates like birthdays and special occasions to cultivate a strong client relationship.

Yoga Studio

For teachers seeking opportunities to teach in group settings and public classes at yoga studios, there are several proactive steps to take:

Research and compile a list of yoga studios in your area. Contact the studios directly to inquire about teaching opportunities. Introduce yourself, express your interest, and inquire about their hiring process. Attend classes at these studios to become familiar with their teaching style, atmosphere, and community. Engage with the studio community by participating in events, workshops, and social gatherings. Build relationships with other teachers and students. Offer to substitute teach classes when needed. This allows you to showcase your teaching style and build rapport with the studio staff. Consider offering donation-based or community classes to gain teaching experience and exposure. Attend auditions or open calls for new teachers at studios. Prepare a short demonstration of your teaching style and philosophy. Volunteer your time and expertise for special events, charity classes, or community outreach programs organized by the studio.

Once you start teaching in a yoga studio, establishing a welcoming atmosphere for students is key. Introduce yourself to new students before class, offering a warm greeting and an invitation to ask any questions. Take the time to learn their names, fostering a sense of connection and community. Be approachable and open to feedback, encouraging students to reach out with any concerns. Keep the students engaging by announcing the focus of your upcoming classes, sparking interest and encouraging return visits. By fostering a friendly and supportive environment, you can enhance the yoga studio experience and cultivate lasting relationships with your students.

Virtual

Best practices for teaching yoga virtually include several key steps to ensure a smooth and professional experience for both you and your students. First, sign in at least 15 minutes prior to the start of your class to set up your equipment and familiarize yourself with the virtual platform. Choose a well-lit area for your practice space and angle your camera appropriately to ensure clear visibility of your movements. Consider cleaning up your background or using a virtual background to minimize distractions. Disable your screensaver and keep your computer plugged in to avoid any interruptions during the class.

Be mindful of any unnecessary noises that may be picked up by your microphone, such as drinking, sniffling, or reading. These distractions can disrupt the flow of the class and detract from the overall experience for your students.

When joining the meeting room, display your full name and title to establish your identity as the instructor. If you plan to use music during your class, ensure that your computer sound is shared so that students can hear it. Introduce yourself warmly and be friendly, just as you would in an in-person class, to create a welcoming atmosphere. After class, make yourself available to answer any questions and connect with your students, fostering a sense of community despite the virtual format.

By following these best practices, you can deliver high-quality virtual yoga classes that engage and inspire your students.

Your Value - How to Charge

Yoga teachers often struggle with charging for their services, sometimes due to conflicting beliefs that spiritual practices should be free. However, understanding the law of abundance and valuing their expertise is pivotal. By recognizing their worth and the transformation they facilitate, teachers can confidently set fair prices. This mindset shift allows them to sustain themselves financially while continuing to serve their communities with integrity and authenticity. Determining your value and how much to charge as a yoga teacher can depend on various factors such as your experience, location, the type of class or service offered, and the demand in your area. Here's a breakdown:

Corporate Classes: Typically higher price ranges, charged per session or per employee, rates can vary based on the size of the company and the frequency of classes. Offering packages such as 10% less for 10 classes, generates recurring revenue.

Studio Classes: Generally at the lower end price range. Studios often pay teachers a set rate per class or offer a percentage of the class revenue. Rates can vary widely depending on the studio's location, reputation, and clientele.

Workshops: Workshops can be a good source of revenue. They are usually priced per ticket sold and the profit split between the teacher and event host/location/studio.

Private Sessions: Typically higher price ranges, and charged upfront. Private sessions are charged at an hourly rate, and charged per attendee. Offering packages such as 10% less for 10 classes, generates recurring revenue.

Packages: Offer discounted rates for clients who purchase multiple sessions or packages upfront. This encourages commitment and provides value to clients.

Donations: For donation-based classes, suggest a recommended donation amount while allowing attendees to contribute what they can afford. This model can be used for community classes or events. It is usually not the most profitable financially but can help build a new teacher's reputation.

Video Content: If offering online classes or video content, consider monthly subscription-based models, pay-per-view options, or tiered membership levels with different pricing and benefits. This offers a passive source of revenue.

Insurance, Waivers, and Invoicing

Insurance

Yoga teachers should invest in liability insurance to protect themselves from potential legal claims in case of accidents or injuries during classes. This coverage provides financial protection and peace of mind, ensuring that teachers can focus on teaching without worrying about potential liabilities. Yoga Alliance offers affordable insurance for yoga instructors.

Waivers

Using waivers is a common practice in the yoga industry to outline the risks associated with participating in classes and to clarify responsibilities for both teachers and students. By having participants sign waivers, teachers can mitigate legal liabilities and establish clear expectations for participation.

Invoicing

Creating and sending invoices is an essential aspect of managing the financial side of a yoga teaching business. Invoices detail the services provided, the cost of those services, and payment terms. By invoicing promptly and accurately, yoga teachers can ensure they are compensated fairly for their time and expertise.

Ethics

Yoga teachers often find themselves in a position where students may seek advice beyond the scope of yoga practice. While it's natural for students to share personal issues and seek guidance, it's essential for yoga teachers to maintain professional boundaries. Yoga teachers are not therapists or trained professionals in areas such as medicine or psychology. Offering advice beyond one's expertise can pose a liability and potentially harm the student. It's important for teachers to gently redirect students to appropriate professionals or resources when faced with issues beyond the realm of yoga practice. By encouraging students to seek help from qualified professionals, yoga teachers can ensure the safety and well-being of their students while honoring the boundaries of their role as yoga instructors.

Ensure the well-being of clients is the top priority, respecting all individuals regardless of race, nationality, gender, sexual orientation, political views, or social and financial status. Refrain from discussing religious or political topics. Maintain truthfulness in interactions, accurately representing your training and experience relevant to meditation teaching. Respect client confidentiality. Abstain from substance use during sessions. Refrain from giving medical advice. Adhere to studio policies for private clients. Uphold a strict anti-harassment policy, avoiding any behavior perceived as inappropriate. Obtain consent before touching clients, especially in classes involving physical contact. Maintain healthy boundaries, avoiding dating clients and inappropriate jokes or behavior. Stay composed and grounded in unexpected situations, seeking help if necessary. Exercise caution, leaving if feeling unsafe, and avoid personal exchanges like car rides or phone numbers unless business-related.

The Seat of the Teacher

Holding the seat of the teacher involves embodying the essence of yoga and serving as a source of inspiration, knowledge, and support for students on their yoga journey. As a yoga teacher, embark on a journey of self-discovery through self-study, diving deep into understanding yourself and your unique voice. Embrace a dedicated spiritual practice to stay connected and elevate your energy, fostering a sense of inner peace and alignment. Follow your passions and pursue what brings you joy, allowing your authentic self to shine through in your teaching. Prioritize building a supportive community grounded in authenticity and genuine connections, steering away from transactional approaches. Maintain consistency and strive for excellence in all aspects of your teaching journey, recognizing that your actions shape your brand and reputation. Remember, the world eagerly awaits your contributions and gifts, urging you to share them with compassion and purpose.

Holding Space

As a yoga teacher, holding space for others is about creating a safe and supportive environment where students feel comfortable being themselves. It's adopting a "come as you are" approach, welcoming students with open arms and without judgment. Part of holding space involves recognizing that students may bring with them difficult emotions, trauma, or heavy experiences. While it is never the role of a yoga teacher to get involved in the student's personal affairs or offer misqualified advice, in these moments, it's important to offer compassion, empathy, and understanding. As teachers, we honor the vulnerability of our students and provide a nurturing space for them to explore and release these emotions through their practice. Holding space means being present, listening without interruption, and offering gentle guidance and support when needed. It's about creating a container where students feel seen, heard, and accepted exactly as they are.

Asana and The Path to a Healthy Practice

My intention in developing Yogi Maha Method was to help you create a lifelong healthy practice that promotes your overall well-being. You might have seen the yogis in India practice until they are around 100 years old; yoga is about longevity and living a long and healthy life. Over the course of my life teaching yoga, I have witnessed people practice yoga from a place that lacks wisdom and mindful body awareness. In this day and age of social media and impressive images of complicated yoga poses that are designed merely to gain traction (not to help you be healthy) yoga asana has lost its potency and deeper healing benefits.

This is actually how people can get injured easily. In the same way that you see professional athletes retiring at a young age because the demand of intense physical training is not sustainable for the body in the long run.

Yoga is a visceral experience, and can be challenging but should never feel painful. The success of a yoga pose should never be evaluated based on aesthetics, how far and impressive it looks; it is never a performance, it's about presence. It's about how deep your presence is inside the container of your sacred body. My hope for you is that this next chapter helps you establish a foundational knowledge of the proper physical alignment of each pose, the benefits and contradictions, and the key to a healthy and lifelong practice. This will help you in your own personal practice because the more evolved you are in your practice as a practitioner, the more masterful you become at teaching yoga to your students.

Synchronizing the breath with movement is fundamental in yoga. Using your breath as a tool supports stability and alignment in poses. Inhaling often corresponds with expanding or lifting, while exhaling corresponds with contracting or grounding. By paying attention to your breath, you can adjust the pace and depth of your movements, ensuring that you practice in a safe and sustainable way for your body. In transitions, linking breath with movement helps you create fluid and graceful transitions between poses while in the flow part of the practice. Allowing your breath to guide you and serve as your fuel. It facilitates the flow of prana throughout your body and is the secret ingredient to dropping into a transcendental state.

As you learned in previous chapters, yoga, first and foremost, is meditation. Anchoring your mind in your breath allows your energy to be more potent and channeled more effectively. Two people can be in the same yoga class, practicing the same poses, and will not equally benefit. If you focus on nothing, you become distracted by everything. If your eyes wander across the yoga room, looking around, copying whatever everyone else is doing, comparing and competing, your energy becomes fragmented and distracted.

This is one of the many unique qualities of Yogi Maha Method and one of the fundamental reasons why my teaching method emphasizes using verbal cues instead of ongoing visual demonstration of the poses by the yoga teacher. If you are constantly looking at the teacher for guidance, your conscious awareness will be focused externally and not internally, and therefore you are no longer in meditation. This hinders you from receiving the deeper and more holistic benefits of a yoga practice. Moreover, looking around is very dangerous for the muscles of the neck, especially when practicing inversions and advanced poses.

Most people are not aware of their body—"Where is my left elbow, right ankle, sternum?" and can find this approach challenging in the beginning. The teacher needs to be sure to encourage them by clearly communicating the long-term benefits of this method. Listening to the cues auditory enhances your mind-body awareness -by strengthening the neurological signals from the brain down to the body part that is worked on- and is the first step to somatic healing and mastery of the sensations of the body. You learn how to control your body instead of your body controlling you. Yoga is an inward and intimate journey; it's you and you alone. I highly recommend softening the gaze or, if possible and safe, closing the eyes completely in gentle poses like downward facing dog, child pose, and especially in savasana.

The alignment poses provided in the next chapter guide you through one side. However, the poses are intended to be practiced on both sides of the body, following the same steps, to ensure equilibrium and balance. Remember to cultivate patience and deep compassion towards yourself while practicing these poses. One person's medicine can be another person's poison; it is never a "one size fits all" approach. Yoga is the practice of inquiry and exploration; it takes time to develop knowledge and understanding of your unique anatomy.

ASANA YOGA POSES

Neutral Rotation Standing Poses

The neutral rotations of the frontal hip bones are pivotal in determining the placement of the feet in neutral rotation standing poses. When the hip bones are facing straight ahead - like car headlights - neither rotated forward nor backward, they provide a reference for aligning the feet.

All alignment instructions provided in this book are for the right side. In yoga practice, we often start with the right side, which is a tradition in many yoga classes. However, it is essential to always perform these poses on both sides to maintain balance in the body.

After completing the pose on the right side, please ensure you repeat the same pose on the left side, following the same alignment. Practicing on both sides will help you achieve a well-rounded and balanced practice, promoting symmetry and strength in your body.

Mountain Pose | Tadasana

tah-dah-sah-nah

Starting Position

Begin standing with your feet together or hip-width apart.
Lift and spread your toes wide and gently place them back down. Ground down evenly through all four corners of your feet, feeling the connection to the earth beneath you.

Proper Alignment

- **Feet**: Root your feet down to the earth, distributing your weight evenly across the balls and heels. Lift the arches and engage the inner thighs.
- **Knees**: Keep a soft bend in your knees to avoid locking them. Engage your quadriceps gently to lift your kneecaps.
- **Legs**: Firm your thigh muscles and rotate them slightly inward.
- **Hips**: Tuck your tailbone slightly, lengthening your spine. Tuck your tailbone, engaging Mula Bandha (root lock), feeling the stability and support in your core.
- **Torso**: Lengthen your spine, lifting through the crown of your head. Imagine a string pulling you up from the top of your head, elongating your spine.
- **Arms**: Let your arms hang naturally by your sides, palms facing forward, fingers extended and energized.
- **Shoulders**: Draw your shoulder blades down and back, opening your chest.
- **Gaze (Drishti):** Keep your chin parallel to the ground, looking straight ahead with a soft, focused gaze.

Modifications

- **Alternating Position**: If balancing is challenging, stand with your feet hip-width apart to create a more stable base.

124

Upward Salute | Urdhva Hastasana
oord-vuh hah-stah-sah-nah

Starting Position
Begin in Tadasana (Mountain Pose).
Ground through your feet and engage your legs.
Sweep your arms out to the sides and overhead, reaching toward the sky.

Proper Alignment
- **Feet**: Ground down evenly through all four corners of your feet, lifting the arches and engaging the inner thighs, feeling the connection to the earth beneath you.
- **Legs**: Engage your quadriceps and lift your kneecaps, feeling your legs strong and active.
- **Hips**: Tuck your tailbone slightly, drawing your lower belly in to engage your core, activating Mula Bandha.
- **Torso**: Lengthen your spine, lifting through the crown of your head.
- **Arms**: Sweep your arms up to the sky, keeping them shoulder-width apart, or have your palms touch. Reach through your fingertips, feeling the energy extending upwards.
- **Hands**: Palms face each other or touch if flexibility allows. Keep your fingers active and energized.
- **Shoulders**: Relax your shoulders away from your ears.
- **Gaze (Drishti):** If it is comfortable for your neck, look up towards your hands. Otherwise, keep your gaze forward.

Modifications
- **Shoulder Relief**: If raising your arms overhead is uncomfortable, you can also keep your fingertips and palms shoulder-distance apart instead of touching.

Contraindications and Risks
- **Shoulder and Neck Tension**: Contraindicated for students with shoulder injuries.

Standing Forward Fold | Uttanasana

oot-tan-ahs-ah-nah

Starting Position

Begin in Tadasana (Mountain Pose).

Reach your arms up overhead, lengthening through your spine.

Hinge at your hips, folding forward with a long spine, leading with your chest.

Proper Alignment

- **Feet**: Ground down through your feet, either hip-width apart or together. Shift your weight into the balls of your feet, stacking the hips above the heels.
- **Knees**: Keep a slight bend in your knees to avoid locking them. Engage your quadriceps to protect your hamstrings.
- **Hips**: Hinge at your hips, leading with your chest as you fold forward. Maintain length in your spine.
- **Torso**: Allow your torso to hang down naturally, feeling a gentle stretch in your hamstrings and lower back. Pull your navel in, activating Uddiyana Bandha, and lift the lower pelvic floor, activating Mula Bandha.
- **Arms**: Let your arms dangle freely or hold opposite elbows, creating space and relaxation in your shoulders.
- **Head**: Let your head hang heavy, releasing tension in your neck. Lengthen the crown of the head toward the floor.

Modifications

- **Using Props**: Place your hands on blocks or your shins for support.
- **Slight Bend**: Add a slight knee bend to avoid rounding your back.
- **Back Issues**: Keep your knees bent and avoid rounding your back excessively.
- **Hamstring Injuries**: Bend your knees or use blocks underneath the hands.

Contraindications and Risks

- **Specific Medical Needs**: If you have high blood pressure, sinus pressure, or eye pain, proceed cautiously and consider modifications.

Half Forward Fold | Ardha Uttanasana

ard-ha oot-tan-ahs-ah-nah

Starting Position
Begin in Uttanasana (Forward Fold).
Lift the chest halfway up with a flat back, extending your spine forward.
Place your palms on your shins.

Proper Alignment
- **Feet**: Ground down through your feet, hip-width apart or together.
- **Knees**: Keep the legs straight as the inner thighs rotate inward, and the kneecaps continue to draw up toward the hips.
- **Hips**: Hinge at your hips, engaging Mula Bandha to extend your spine forward. Shift your weight slightly forward to stack your sit bones directly over your heels.
- **Torso**: Lift halfway up with a flat back, feeling length through your spine. Engage Uddiyana Bandha to draw the belly slightly in and toward the spine.
- **Arms**: Place your hands on your shins, thighs, or blocks.
- **Head**: Reach the crown of the head forward, away from the hips, and away from the tailbone, taking out all rounding in the spine.
- **Gaze (Drishti):** Look slightly down to maintain a length in the back of the neck, creating a straight line from your head to your tailbone.

Modifications
- **Using Props**: Keep your hands on your thighs or blocks to support your back and maintain a flat spine.

Contraindications and Risks
- **Back Injuries**: Contraindicated for students with back pain.

Plank Pose | Phalakasana
fal-ahk-ah-sah-nah

Starting Position
Begin in Ardha Uttanasana (Half Forward Fold).
Place your palms on the mat shoulder-width apart.
Step your feet to the back of the mat, arriving at the top of a push-up.

Proper Alignment
- **Feet**: Step your feet back, hip-width apart. Press the balls of your feet into the mat, engaging your legs.
- **Legs**: Engage your quadriceps. Activate the inner thigh muscles by spiraling them upward to the sky.
- **Hips**: Maintain a neutral spine, avoiding sagging or lifting the hips too high. Lengthen the tailbones toward the heels.
- **Torso**: Draw your belly in and engage your abdominal muscles. Engage your core to support your lower back, activating Uddiyana Bandha (abdominal lock).
- **Arms**: Stack your shoulders directly over your wrists, keeping your arms straight and strong. Press firmly into the mat,
- **Hands**: Spread your fingers wide, pressing down evenly through your palms, activating Hasta Bandha.
- **Gaze (Drishti):** Look slightly ahead of your fingertips to open the chest. Keep the back of the neck long and neutral, aligning your cervical spine with the rest of your spine.

129

Modifications

- **Resting Forearms**: If you have wrist weakness or pain, you can modify this pose by resting your forearms on your mat and keeping your shoulders stacked over your elbows.
- **Core Strength**: If you are still building strength for this posture, consider dropping your knees to the mat while maintaining a straight line from head to hips.

Contraindications and Risks

- **Wrist Problems**: Contraindicated for students with wrist weakness or pain.

Four Limb Staff Pose | Chaturanga Dandasana
chah-tur-ang-guh dun-dahs-ah-nah

Starting Position
Begin in Phalakasana (Plank Pose).
Shift your weight onto the tips of your toes, moving your shoulders beyond the wrists. Bend your elbows, stacking them directly above your wrists, hugging your elbows into your body.

Proper Alignment
- **Feet**: Keep your feet hip-width apart, pressing the balls of your feet into the mat. Engage your legs to maintain stability.
- **Legs**: Firm your quadriceps and spiral the inner thighs toward the sky.
- **Hips**: Maintain a neutral spine, avoiding sagging or lifting your hips too high.
- **Torso**: Draw your belly in and engage your abdominal muscles to support your lower back, activating Uddiyana Bandha. Lower your body towards the mat, keeping a straight line from head to heels.
- **Arms**: Bend your elbows to a 90-degree angle, keeping them close to your body. Your upper arms should be parallel to the mat.
- **Shoulders**: Slide the shoulders down the back as your shoulder blades press into the back and widen away from the spine. Draw the chest forward and spread the collar bones wide.
- **Hands**: Spread your fingers wide, pressing down evenly through all four corners of your palms, activating Hasta Bandha. Keep your wrists stacked directly under your elbows.
- **Gaze (Drishti):** Look slightly ahead of your fingertips to keep your chest open and your neck long and neutral, aligning your cervical spine with the rest of your spine.

Modifications

- **Modified Chaturanga**: Lower your knees to the mat while maintaining a straight line from head to knees.
- **Wrist Issues**: Modify by doing a Forearm Plank to reduce strain on your wrists.
- **Shoulder Injuries**: Avoid lowering too deeply and keep your elbows close to your body to protect your shoulders.
- **Lower Back Pain**: Engage your core and maintain a neutral spine to support your lower back.

Contraindications and Risks

- **Pregnancy**: Contraindicated for pregnant students.

Forearm Plank

Starting Position
Begin in Plank Pose (Phalakasana).
Lower one forearm at a time to the mat, stacking your shoulders over your elbows.
Engage your core and maintain a straight line from head to heels.

Proper Alignment
- **Feet**: Keep your feet hip-width apart, pressing the balls of your feet into the mat. Engage your legs for stability.
- **Legs**: Engage your quadriceps and hug the inner thighs inwards and up.
- **Hips**: Maintain a neutral spine, avoiding sagging or lifting your hips too high.
- **Torso**: Draw your belly in and engage your abdominal muscles to support your lower back, activating Uddiyana Bandha. Keep your body in a straight line from the back of the head to the heels.
- **Arms**: Place your forearms parallel on the mat, shoulder-width apart. Press down through your forearms and place your palms on the mat, activating Hasta Bandha. Students can interlace their hands for more stability.
- **Shoulders**: Slide your shoulders down your back as your shoulder blades press into the back and widen away from the spine. Draw your chest forward and spread your collarbones wide.
- **Gaze (Drishti)**: Look slightly ahead of your fingertips to keep your collarbone broad and neck extended and neutral, aligning your cervical spine with the rest of your spine.

Modifications
- **Avoiding Wrist Pain**: Rest your knees on the mat and slide them behind the hips, keeping your chest open.

Contraindications and Risks
- **Shoulder Injuries**: Contraindicated for students with shoulder injuries.

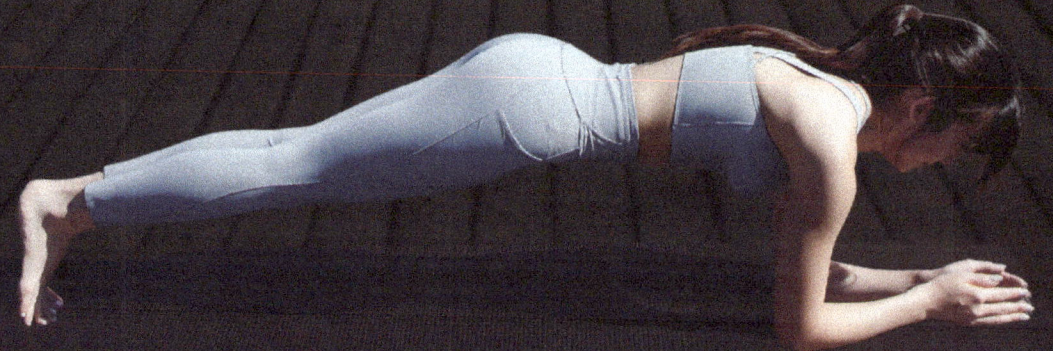

Sunbird Pose

Starting Position
Begin in Tabletop Position.
Inhale: Lift and extend one leg and your opposite arm to be parallel with your mat, maintaining a long and straight line.
Exhale: Option to hold this pose or contract, bringing the extended elbow and knee together to touch.

Proper Alignment
- **Feet**: Flex your right foot, pressing through the heel to engage the leg muscles, and keep your toes facing down.
- **Legs**: Engage your quadriceps and glutes to lift your leg parallel to the mat. Keep your hips square and in a neutral rotation. Spiral the inner thigh up.
- **Hips**: Maintain a neutral rotation, avoiding sagging or lifting your hips too high.
- **Torso**: Draw your belly in and engage your abdominal muscles to support your lower back, activating Uddiyana Bandha. Keep your body in a straight line from the back of the head to the heel.
- **Shoulders**: Draw the shoulder of your lifted left arm down your back.
- **Arms**: Extend your left arm forward, parallel to the mat, with your thumb pointing up.
- **Gaze (Drishti):** Look down toward the floor to keep the back of your neck long and neutral, aligning your cervical spine with the rest of your spine.

Modifications
- **Knee pain or injury**: If you have knee pain or injury, consider placing a blanket under your knees for support.

Contraindications and Risks
- **Wrist pain**: Avoid this pose if you have wrist pain.

Chair Pose | Utkatasana

oot-kah-tah-sah-nah

Starting Position

Begin in Tadasana (Mountain Pose).

Reach your arms up overhead, lengthening through your spine.

Bend your knees and sit your hips back as if getting ready to sit into a chair.

Proper Alignment

- **Feet**: Keep your feet hip-width apart or together, sending your weight back into the heels and staying light on the toes.
- **Legs**: Bend your knees deeply, keeping them in line with your toes. Avoid letting your knees go past your toes.
- **Hips**: Sit your hips back and down as if sitting in a chair. Keep your weight in your heels. Engage Mula Bandha to support your core.
- **Torso**: Lengthen your spine by tucking the tailbone slightly underneath and inward. Keep your chest lifted and your shoulders relaxed. Lift through the crown of your head.
- **Arms**: Reach your arms up overhead, keeping them shoulder-width apart. Extend through the upper arms with the palms facing each other as if holding a ball of light. Rotate the pinky fingers toward each other while sliding the shoulders down the back.
- **Gaze (Drishti)**: Look forward. Keep your neck long and neutral.

Modifications

- **Widening Stance**: Keep your feet hip-width apart, and place a yoga block between the inner thighs to reduce knee strain. Sit back less deeply to reduce intensity.

Contraindications and Risks

- **Knee Issues**: If you have knee problems, avoid deep knee bends. Keep your weight in your heels and ensure your knees align with your toes.
- **Lower Back Pain**: Engage your core and maintain a neutral spine to support your lower back. Tuck the tailbone slightly underneath and inward to avoid overarching your back.
- **Pregnant**: Contraindicated for students who are pregnant. Proceed with caution.
- **Shoulder Injuries**: Modify the arm position to avoid discomfort. Bend your elbows or keep your hands in a prayer position.

Warrior I | Virabhadrasana I

veer-ah-bah-drah-sah-nah

Starting Position

Begin in Adho Mukha Svanasana (Downward Facing Dog).

- Lift your right leg to the sky to a three-legged Downward Facing Dog.
- Step your right foot forward to the top of your mat, pivot your left foot flat, and point your left toes slightly forward toward the front of the mat. Sweep your arms up to the sky.

Proper Alignment

- **Feet**: Step your right foot forward between your hands, ensuring your toes are pointing straight toward the front of the mat. Seal the back edge of your left foot into the mat and point your left toes slightly forward to square your left hip forward. Your feet should be hip-distance apart.
- **Legs**: Bend your right knee to a 90-degree angle, keeping it directly over your ankle. Straighten your left leg and spiral the inner thigh back. Press the outer edge of your left foot into the mat.
- **Hips**: Square your hips towards the front of the mat. Draw your right hip back and your left hip forward.
- **Pelvis**: Tuck your tailbone slightly to maintain a neutral pelvis and engage Mula Bandha to support your core. Pull your navel inward to avoid overarching your lower back.
- **Torso**: Lift your torso up, extending your spine. Keep your chest lifted and your shoulders relaxed.
- **Arms**: Raise your arms overhead, keeping the biceps by the ears. Reach through your fingertips.
- **Hands**: Palms face each other or touch if flexibility allows. Keep your shoulders relaxed away from your ears.
- **Gaze (Drishti):** Look straight ahead or up towards your hands if comfortable for your neck.

Modifications

- **Alternative Pose:** Separate the palms wider than the shoulders, and keep your hands on your hips or in prayer if you have high blood pressure or a history of heart disease.

Contraindications and Risks

- **Specific Medical Needs**: Contraindicated for students with high blood pressure or a history of heart disease. Proceed with caution and consider modification.

Humble Warrior | Baddha Virabhadrasana

bah-dah veer-ah-bah-drah-sah-nah

Starting Position

Begin in Virabhadrasana I (Warrior I).

Interlace your fingers behind your back as you lift your chest toward the sky, rolling your shoulders back.

Lean forward and connect the outside edge of your right shoulder to the inside edge of your right knee.

Proper Alignment

- **Feet**: Ensure your right heel aligns with the arch of your left foot. Ground down through the outer edge of your left foot.
- **Legs**: Bend your right knee to a 90-degree angle, keeping it directly over your ankle. Straighten your left leg, pressing firmly into the mat. Activate the inner thigh muscles of both legs by energetically drawing the legs toward the midline.
- **Hips**: Square your hips to the front of your mat.
- **Torso**: Lengthen through your spine, drawing your chest toward your right thigh, as you pull your navel toward your spine, activating Uddiyana Bandha.
- **Arms**: Extend your arms behind you, interlacing your fingers. Reach your hands toward the sky.
- **Head**: Let your head hang to release the neck.
- **Gaze (Drishti):** Rest your gaze softly down toward the mat or slightly back toward your back foot, keeping your neck long and relaxed.

Modifications

- **Using Props**: Use a strap between your hands if you cannot comfortably interlace your fingers.

Contraindications and Risks

- **Shoulder Pain**: Use caution and avoid overextending your shoulders. Modify with a strap if needed.
- **Knee Issues**: Ensure your front knee is aligned over your ankle and avoid placing too much strain on your knee.

Warrior III I Virabhadrasana III
veer-ah-bah-drah-sah-nah

Starting Position
Begin in Tadasana (Mountain Pose).
Bring the hands into prayer Anjali Mudra.
Balancing on the right leg, lean forward and lift your left leg parallel to the floor, and align your torso so that it is parallel with the earth.

Proper Alignment
- **Feet**: Distribute your weight evenly to all four corners of your right foot. Spread your toes and lift the inner arch of your foot. Point your left toes down with your pinky toe aiming toward the mat, and flex your left foot.
- **Legs**: Firm the thigh of your right leg, and keep a micro bend in the knee. Extend firmly through your left leg.
- **Hips**: Spiral your outer left hip toward the floor and your inner left thigh toward the sky so that your frontal hip points are parallel to the mat and the hips are in a neutral rotation.
- **Torso**: Lengthen through your spine, drawing your chest forward as you pull your navel toward your spine, activating Uddiyana Bandha.

- **Arms**: For the full expression of Virabhadrasana III, extend your arms forward with your biceps aligned with your ears and fingertips pointed ahead.
- **Gaze (Drishti):** Rest your gaze comfortably on the floor ahead of your right foot to ensure one line of energy from your extended fingertips to your extended heel.

Modifications
- **Using Props**: Place blocks under your shoulders and use your hands to stabilize the pose until you build more strength.
- **Alternative Pose:** If you have a weaker back, you may extend your arms by your sides with palms facing the sky or keeping hands in Anjali (prayer) at the heart center. For stability, you may also welcome a slight bend to the knee of your standing leg.

Contraindications and Risks
- **High blood pressure**: Contraindicated for students with high blood pressure.
- **Lower back** pain: Proceed with caution and consider using props.
- **Knee injuries**: Proceed with caution and consider using props.

Twisting Half Moon I Parivrtta Ardha Chandrasana

pah-ree-vrit-tah ard-ha chan-drah-sah-nah

Starting Position

Begin in Virabhadrasana III (Warrior III) with your right foot on your mat and your left leg lifted.

Place your left fingertips on the mat directly under your left shoulder.

Rotate your chest toward the right as your right fingertips reach for the sky.

Proper Alignment

- **Feet**: Ground down through your right foot, pressing evenly into the mat. Flex your left foot, pointing your toes toward the mat to maintain a neutral rotation in the hips.
- **Legs**: Hug the inner thigh muscles toward each other. Lift your left leg parallel to the ground, keeping it strong and active.
- **Hips**: Keep the hips in neutral rotation.
- **Torso**: Rotate your chest toward the right as you lengthen through your spine and extend sideways over your right leg.
- **Arms**: Reach your right arm towards the sky. Extend your left arm towards the ground, reaching for a block or the mat.
- **Shoulders**: Draw your shoulder blades away from your spine and lengthen your neck.
- **Hands**: Keep your left hand light on the mat or block. Extend your right hand actively reach towards the sky.
- **Head**: Draw the crown of your head forward.
- **Gaze (Drishti)**: Look up towards your right hand or down at your right foot if your neck is sensitive.

Modifications

- **Using Props**: If your spine is not at level with your hips, place a block under your left hand to lengthen your spine.

Contraindications and Risks

- **Pregnancy**: Contraindicated for students who are pregnant.

Standing Splits | Urdhva Prasarita Eka Padasana

oord-hvah prah-sah-ree-tah eh-kah pah-dah-sah-nah

Starting Position
Beginning in Virabhadrasana III (Warrior III).
Keep your left leg lifted and fold your torso over your right leg, placing your hands on the floor.
Lengthen from the base of your spine, reaching your hands toward the ground.

Proper Alignment
- **Feet:** Maintain an even distribution of weight among all four corners of your right foot while lifting your inner arch.
- **Legs**: Press your right thigh back and firm your right leg.
- **Hips**: Square your frontal hip points toward the floor. Hug the hip of your right leg toward your midline and firm your leg.
- **Arms**: Lower your arms down to the earth.
- **Shoulders**: Slide your shoulder blades down your back.
- **Head**: Drop your head and align your forehead toward your right shin.
- **Hands**: Frame your right leg, or wrap one or both hands behind your right leg to get your forehead closer to your shin.
- **Gaze (Drishti):** Look down and toward the back of the mat, keeping the back of your neck long and relaxed.

Modifications
- Using Props: Use blocks under your hands to reduce strain.
- Alternative Pose: To avoid hyperextension of your standing leg's knee, maintain a subtle bend in the knee.
- Hamstring Injuries: Use caution and avoid overstretching your hamstrings. Modify with blocks or support.

Contraindications and Risks
- **Ankle Pain:** Contraindicated for students with ankle pain.
- **Knee Pain:** Contraindicated for students with knee pain.

Low Lunge | Anjaneyasana
ahn-jah-nay-ah-sah-nah

Starting Position
Begin in Downward Facing Dog (Adho Mukha Svanasana).
Step your right foot forward, aligning your knee directly above your ankle.
Lower your left knee down to the mat. Slide your left knee back so it is behind your sit bones.

Proper Alignment
- **Legs**: Keep your right foot aligned directly underneath your knee, forming a 90-degree angle.
- **Hips**: Engage the glute muscles of your left leg and lift the frontal hip bones off your right thigh. This action lengthens the psoas muscle.
- **Torso**: Tuck your tailbone underneath and inward toward your face. Lift your lower belly up to feel a stretch.

- **Shoulders**: Draw your trapezius muscles down your back to draw your chest forward and broaden your collarbones.
- **Arms**: Reach your arms up toward the sky and lengthen from both sides of your waist. Straighten your arms to lift your chest.
- **Hands**: Keep your hands shoulder-distance apart with your pinky fingers slightly rotating back or bring the hands into Steeple Mudra (hand gesture) by interlacing the fingers but the indexes to point up to the sky.
- **Gaze (Drishti):** Look straight ahead or slightly up towards your thumbs, keeping your neck long and relaxed.

Modifications
- **Using Props**: Use folded blanket underneath your left knee.

Contraindications and Risks
- **Special Medical Needs**: Contraindicated for students with knee injury.

Crescent Pose | Ashta Chandrasana
ahsh-tah chan-drah-sah-nah

Starting Position
Start in Adho Mukha Svanasana (Downward Facing Dog).
Step your right foot forward between your hands, aligning your knee directly above the ankle. Keep your left toes planted and lift your left heel from the mat with the toes pointing straight forward, coming into a runner's lunge.
On an inhale, sweep your arms up to the sky.

147

Proper Alignment

- **Feet**: Feet are hip-distance apart to achieve greater stability.
- **Legs**: Bend your right knee, keeping it aligned over your ankle. Engage the quadriceps muscles of your left leg, keeping it strong and active.
- **Hips**: Square your hips to the front of the mat, maintaining a neutral rotation in the hips. Engage the glute muscles of your left leg and lift the frontal hip bones off your right thigh. This action lengthens the psoas muscle. Tuck your tailbone underneath and inward toward your face.
- **Torso**: Lengthen through your spine and both sides of the waist, lifting your chest towards the sky. Lift your lower belly up and in.
- **Arms**: Extend your arms overhead, reaching through your fingertips. Keep your biceps by your ears.
- **Hands**: Palms face each other as if holding a ball between the hands. Keep your fingers active, reaching towards the sky. Option to interlace the fingers except the index fingers for steeple mudra.
- **Gaze (Drishti):** Look straight ahead or slightly up towards your thumbs, keeping your neck long and relaxed.

Modifications

- **Flexibility**: Keep your back knee slightly bent to reduce strain.
- **Alternative Pose:** Press your palms together overhead.

Contraindications and Risks

- **Knee Injuries**: If you have knee injuries, consider modifying your pose to Anjaneyasana (Low Lunge) with a blanket supporting your back knee on your mat.

Lunging Prayer Twist | Parivrtta Anjaneyasana

pah-ree-vrit-tah ahn-jah-nay-ah-sah-nah

Starting Position

Start in Ashta Chandrasana (Crescent Pose).
Reach your arms a bit higher.
Bring your hands together at the heart center in Anjali Mudra, and place your right elbow outside your left knee.

Proper Alignment

- **Feet**: For stability, your feet should be at least hip-distance apart.
- **Legs**: Bend your left knee, keeping it aligned over your ankle. Resist collapsing your left knee forward. Balance on the toes of your right foot, lift your quadriceps up and spin your inner right thigh up as your leg hugs into your midline.
- **Hips**: Activate your hips by drawing your inner thighs towards each other. Use the muscles of your outer hips to keep your knee pointing straight ahead. Engage your glute muscles.
- **Torso**: Keep your head higher than your heart and your heart higher than your hips, creating a diagonal line and maintaining an uplifted energy in the torso, Udana Vayu. Twist your torso towards your left knee, using your side obliques to deepen the twist as you maintain spinal length.

- **Shoulders**: Stack your shoulders to continually square your hips forward to create a genuine twist. Draw your shoulders down your back.
- **Arms**: Bring your hands to your heart in a prayer position, pressing your palms together. Place your right elbow on the outside edge of your left knee. Stack your elbows directly on top of each other, creating a clear, open line of energy.
- **Hands**: Keep your palms pressed together, creating a connection. Actively press up with your bottom hand to lengthen your bottom ribs and create more space for breath.
- **Gaze (Drishti):** Look over your left shoulder, keeping your neck long and relaxed.

Modifications
- **Flexibility**: Keep your back knee on the mat for added stability.
- **Alternative Pose:** Practice Anjaneyasana (Low Lunge) as a modification.
- **Neck**: Look to the side or down to relieve the neck from unnecessary pressure.

Contraindications and Risks
- **Pregnancy**: Contraindicated for students who are pregnant.

Twisting Triangle Pose | Parivrtta Trikonasana

pah-ree-vrit-tah tree-koh-nah-sah-nah

Starting Position
Start in Trikonasana (Triangle Pose).
Lengthen through your spine, reaching your arms overhead. Place your right hand on your hip.
Hinge from the hips and fold, placing your left hand on the floor or block inside or outside of your right foot.

Proper Alignment
- **Feet**: Align your right heel with the heel of your left foot or separate the inner thighs wider. Ground down through both heels, pressing evenly into the mat.
- **Legs**: Engage your quadriceps and inner thighs, keeping your legs strong and active.
- **Hips**: Maintain neutral rotation in the hips by drawing your right hip back and your left hip forward. Spiral the inseam of your left leg backward and the outseam forward.
- **Torso**: Lengthen through your spine, twisting your torso to the right.
- **Arms**: Reach your left hand to the outside of your right foot. Extend your right arm towards the sky.
- **Hands**: Keep your left-hand light on the mat or block. Extend your right hand actively towards the sky.
- **Gaze (Drishti):** Look up towards your right thumb or down at your left foot if your neck is sensitive.

Modifications
- **Using Props**: Use a block under your left hand to reduce strain.

Contraindications and Risks
- **Pregnancy**: Contraindicated for pregnant students.
- **Neck Injury**: If you have a history of neck injury or have neck muscles that feel tired, you may gaze down or straight ahead.

Twisting Side Angle Pose | Parivrtta Parsvakonasana
pah-ree-vrit-tah parsh-vah-koh-nah-sah-nah

Starting Position
Begin in Virabhadrasana I (Warrior I).
Bring your hands to heart in Anjali Mudra.
Twist your torso toward your right knee, using your side obliques to deepen your twist.
Place your left elbow on the outside edge of your right knee, stacking your elbows directly on top of each other.

Proper Alignment
- **Feet**: Align your right heel with the arch of your left foot. Seal the outer edge of your left foot to the floor as the inner arch lifts and your thigh firms back. Keep the left toes angled slightly forward to the front corner of your mat.
- **Legs**: Keep your right knee aligned directly over your right heel with your right thigh parallel to the floor.
- **Hips**: Actively draw your right hip into your midline.
- **Torso**: Lengthen through your spine, twisting your torso toward your right thigh and up toward the ceiling as your top ribs roll back and bottom ribs roll down.

- **Arms:** Reach your left hand to the outside of your right foot. Extend your right arm towards the sky.
- **Hands:** Place your left hand on the outside edge of your right foot or keep your hands in Anjali Mudra.
- **Gaze (Drishti):** Look up towards your right hand or down at your left foot if your neck is sensitive.

Modifications

- **Using Props:** Use a block under your left hand to reduce strain.
- **Alternative Pose:** If your hip cannot draw in and continues to stick out toward the side of your mat, come into Parivrtta Anjaneyasana (Lunging Prayer Twist) on the back toes instead.

Contraindications and Risks

- **Pregnancy:** Contraindicated for pregnant students.

Eagle Pose | Garudasana

gah-roo-dah-sah-nah

Starting Position

Begin in Tadasana (Mountain Pose).

Lengthen through your spine, reaching your arms overhead.

Bend your knees slightly and cross your right thigh over your left thigh, hooking your right foot behind your left calf.

Cross your left arm over your right arm, bringing your palms together or the backs of your hands together.

Proper Alignment

- **Feet**: Root down through your left foot, pressing evenly into the mat.
- **Legs**: Engage your left leg, keeping it strong and active. Cross your right thigh over your left thigh, hooking your right foot behind your left calf. Press your inner thighs together.
- **Hips**: Draw the right hip back and the left hip forward, maintaining a neutral rotation in the hips. Keep the hips facing the front.
- **Torso**: Lengthen through your spine, keeping your torso upright.
- **Arms**: Cross your left arm over your right arm, bringing your palms together or the backs of your hands together. Stack your elbows, bending both arms at the elbows, and cross your forearms to face each other. Peel your shoulder blades away from the midline. Lift your arm up so that the elbows are in alignment with the shoulders. Draw your forearms away from your face.
- **Head**: Lift through the crown of your head, keeping your neck long and free of tension.
- **Hands**: Spin your palms to face each other.
- **Gaze (Drishti):** Find your focal gaze (drishti) by looking straight ahead, keeping your neck long and relaxed.

Modifications

- **Alternative Pose:** Place your right toes on the mat for stability.
- **Knee Pain**: Use caution and avoid placing too much strain on your knees. Modify with support as needed.

Dancer Pose | Natarajasana

nah-tah-rah-jah-sah-nah

Starting Position

Begin in Mountain Pose (Tadasana).
Lengthen through your spine, reaching your right arm forward.
Bend your left knee, reaching your left hand back to grasp your left foot.
Hinge forward and kick the foot into the hand.

Proper Alignment

- **Feet**: Ground down through your right foot, pressing evenly into the mat. Bend the left knee and hug the heel toward the left glute. Hold the top of the left foot with your left hand. Like a bow and arrow, kick the foot into the hand to stretch the quadricep and open the shoulder.
- **Legs**: Keep the front of your right leg facing the earth. Press your right shin to the back of your mat. Maintain a soft bend in your standing knee.
- **Hips**: Maintain a neutral rotation in the hips. Keep your sacrum parallel to the floor by squaring both your hip points down.
- **Torso**: Keep the chest slightly elevated and leaning forward.
- **Arms**: Extend your right arm forward.
- **Shoulders**: Option to hold the foot from the inner edge, allowing the shoulder to externally rotate. Breathe into your front body to expand your chest.
- **Hands**: Face your right palm upward as you reach through your fingertips or, option to bring the thumb and index fingers to connect for Gyan Mudra (hand gesture). Hold your left foot with your left hand.
- **Gaze (Drishti)**: Look straight ahead, focusing your gaze softly on a fixed point in front of you (Drishti) to help maintain balance, keeping your neck long and relaxed.

Modifications

- **Using Props**: Use a strap around your left foot if you cannot reach your foot comfortably.

Contraindications and Risks

- **Special Medical Needs**: contraindicated for students with herniated or bulged discs.

Wide Leg Forward Fold A | Prasarita Padottanasana A

prah-sah-ree-tah pah-doh-tah-nah-sah-nah

Starting Position

Begin in Mountain Pose (Tadasana).

Step your feet wide apart, turning your toes slightly in.

Hinge forward from your hips, bringing your hands to the mat or blocks.

Proper Alignment

- **Feet**: Keep your feet wide apart without collapsing down, turning your toes slightly in. Distribute your weight through all four corners of your feet.
- **Legs**: Engage your quadriceps and inner thighs, keeping your legs strong and active.
- **Hips**: Hinge forward from your hips, lengthening through your spine. Tilt your sit bones over your shoulders, engaging Uddiyana Bandha and Mula Bandha.
- **Torso**: Lower your chest towards the mat, lengthening through your spine.
- **Arms**: Extend your arms down towards the mat, reaching for the ground,
- **Head**: Allow the crown of your head to drop toward the floor, lengthening the muscles of your neck.
- **Hands**: Rest your hands on the mat or yoga blocks, with the option to hold your ankles or hook the two peace fingers around the big toes.
- **Gaze (Drishti):** Look down and back, keeping your neck long and relaxed.

Modifications

- **Using Props**: Use blocks under your hands to reduce strain.
- **Alternative Pose:** You are welcome to rest the crown of your head on the floor without hyperextending your inner thighs.
- **Lower Back Pain**: Engage your core to support your lower back and avoid rounding.

Contraindications and Risks

- **Medical complications:** Contraindicated for students with high blood pressure, acid reflux, or hernia.

Wide Leg Forward Fold B | Prasarita Padottanasana B

prah-sah-ree-tah pah-doh-tah-nah-sah-nah

Starting Position

Begin in Prasarita Padottanasana B (Wide Leg Forward B).
Keep your hands on your hips, and hug the elbows toward each other as your torso folds forward.

Wide Leg Forward Fold C | Prasarita Padottanasana C

prah-sah-ree-tah pah-doh-tah-nah-sah-nah

Starting Position

Begin in Prasarita Padottanasana A (Wide Leg Forward A).
Interlace your hands behind your lower back, drawing your palms together as your torso folds forward. To avoid hyperextension, welcome a micro bend to your elbows.
Lift your shoulder heads away from the floor and spread your collarbones across your chest while drawing your shoulder blades toward your spine.

Wide Leg Forward Fold D | Prasarita Padottanasana D

prah-sah-ree-tah pah-doh-tah-nah-sah-nah

Starting Position

Begin in Prasarita Padottanasana A (Wide Leg Forward A).
Hook your index fingers around your big toes as your torso folds forward.
Bend your elbows into a 90-degree angle, drawing your chest toward the space between your legs, and slide your shoulder blades down your back.

160

Pyramid Pose | Parsvottanasana

parsh-voh-tah-nah-sah-nah

Starting Position

Begin in Tadasana (Mountain Pose).
Step your left foot back, keeping your feet hip-width apart.
Hinge forward from your hips, folding forward over your right leg.

Proper Alignment

- Feet: Keep your feet hip-width apart, pressing evenly into the mat. Turn your back foot slightly forward, allowing your back toes to point almost ahead. Press your back heel firmly into the earth.
- Legs: Lift the quadriceps muscle away from the knee. Hug your inner thighs toward each other, keeping both legs straight. You can keep a soft bend in the front knee.
- Hips: Draw your right hip back and your left hip forward. Fold forward at your hips and maintain a neutral hip placement by spiraling the inseam of the left leg back while wrapping the outseam of the left leg forward.
- Torso: Lengthen through your spine, lowering your chest towards your front leg.
- Arms: Extend your arms down towards the mat, reaching for the ground or blocks.

161

- **Shoulders**: Draw your shoulders away from your ears and lengthen your neck.
- **Hands**: Place your hands on the mat or yoga blocks, pressing gently to deepen the stretch.
- **Gaze (Drishti)**: Look down and back, keeping your neck long and relaxed.

Modifications

- **Alternative Pose:** Avoid hyperextending your front leg, keep it slightly bent by gently pressing the top of the front calf forward.

Contraindications and Risks

- **Hamstring Injuries**: Place two yoga blocks underneath the hands and stack the hands directly underneath the shoulders.
- **Medical Complications**: Contraindicated for students with high blood pressure or a history of stroke or glaucoma.

Hand to Big Toe Pose I | Utthita Hasta Padangusthasana I

oot-hee-tah hahs-tah pah-dahn-goos-tah-sah-nah

Starting Position
Begin in Mountain Pose (Tadasana).
Lift your right knee towards your chest, holding your right big toe with your right hand. Extend your right leg forward, and extend the leg toward straight.

Proper Alignment
- **Feet**: Point the left toes straight forward and press through all four corners of the foot. Keep the sole of your right foot facing directly ahead.
- **Legs**: Draw your right knee into your chest toward your midline and hook your first two fingers around your right big toe. Use a strap if needed. When ready, extend your right leg toward straight, continuing to draw your toes back toward your face. Keep your left leg straight.
- **Hips**: Level both hips with each other so that your waistline is even. Maintain an even length through both sides of your waist by lowering the femur of your extended right leg toward the floor.
- **Torso**: Draw your front ribs down. Engage your abdominal muscles and lift the low pelvic floor, activating Uddiyana Bandha and Mula Bandha.
- **Shoulders**: Stack your shoulders over your hips. Hug the shoulder of your extended arm back into your shoulder joint as both shoulders relax down your back and widen through the collarbones.
- **Hands**: Place your left hand on your left hip bone and hook your two peace fingers around your right big toe.
- **Head**: Reach the crown of your head toward the sky, keeping your chin parallel to the floor. Elongate both sides of your neck.
- **Gaze (Drishti)**: Gaze directly ahead with a focused gaze (drishti), keeping your neck long and relaxed.

Modifications
- **Balancing Support**: Use a wall or recline on the floor for support.
- **Using Props**: Use a strap around your foot if you cannot reach your big toe comfortably.

Contraindications and Risks
- **Balance Issues**: Practice near a wall or with support until you build more confidence and stability.

Hand to Big Toe Pose III | Utthita Hasta Padangusthasana III

oot-hee-tah hahs-tah pah-dahn-goos-tah-sah-nah

Starting Position

Start in Utthita Hasta Padangusthasana I (Hand to Big Toe Pose I).

Switch the grip of your hands, and hold the outer edge of your right foot with your left hand.

Extend your right arm back coming into a spinal twist.

Drop the shoulders away from the ears and lengthen your spine.

Modifications

- **Using Props**: Modify by using a strap if you have tight hamstrings.

Contraindications and Risks

- **Hamstring Injuries**: Use caution and avoid overstretching your hamstrings. Modify with a strap if needed.
- **Pregnancy**: Contraindicated during pregnancy.

165

Externally Rotated Standing Poses

Externally rotated standing poses in yoga involve turning the legs and feet outward from the center of the body. This rotation typically originates from the hips and can affect the entire lower body, including the thighs, knees, and ankles.

All alignment instructions provided in this book are for the right side. In yoga practice, we often start with the right side, which is a tradition in many yoga classes. However, it is essential to always perform these poses on both sides to maintain balance in the body.

After completing the pose on the right side, please ensure you repeat the same pose on the left side, following the same alignment. Practicing on both sides will help you achieve a well-rounded and balanced practice, promoting symmetry and strength in your body.

Warrior II | Virabhadrasana II

veer-ah-bah-drah-sah-nah

Starting Position

Begin in Virabhadrasana I (Warrior I) with your right foot forward.

Spread your arms, reaching your right arm toward the front of the mat and your left arm toward the back.

Align your right heel with the arch of your left foot.

Proper Alignment

- **Feet**: Point the right toes straight ahead. Ensure your right heel aligns with the arch of your left foot as if standing on a tight rope. Ground down through the outer edge of your left foot.
- **Legs**: Bend your right knee to a 90-degree angle, keeping it directly over your ankle. Straighten your left leg, pressing firmly into the mat. Activate your inner thigh muscles of both legs by energetically drawing your legs toward the midline.
- **Hips**: Externally rotate your right hip by spiraling its outer side underneath and in, to stack the knee above the ankle. Internally rotate your left hip. Align your pelvis with the long edge of the mat. Pull the navel in toward the spine, activating Uddiyana Bandha and lift your low pelvic floor activating Mula Bandha to support your lower back.
- **Torso**: Extend your torso sideways and keep it upright, lengthening through the spine. Stack the head above the shoulders and the shoulders above the hips, keeping a straight line from head to tail.

167

- **Arms**: Extend your arms away from the spine and to the sides, parallel to the floor. Reach through your fingertips, creating energy in your arms.
- **Shoulders**: Stack the shoulders directly over the hips. Soften the shoulders down and away from the ears.
- **Hands**: Palms face down.
- **Gaze (Drishti)**: Look over your right middle finger with a focused gaze.

Contraindications and Risks

- **Knee Alignment:** Cautiously proceed and externally rotate the front hip by spiraling its outer side underneath and inward to make sure your front knee does not collapse inward. Ensure your front knee is aligned with your ankle, pointing directly ahead.

Reverse Warrior | Viparita Virabhadrasana
vee-pah-ree-tah veer-ah-bah-drah-sah-nah

Starting Position
Begin in Virabhadrasana II (Warrior II) with your right foot forward.
Flip your right palm up, and lift the arm towards the sky.
Rest your left hand lightly on your left thigh with your palm facing down.

Proper Alignment

- **Feet**: Maintain the alignment of Warrior II, grounding down through both feet.
- **Legs**: Keep your right knee bent to a 90-degree angle and your left leg straight.
- **Hips**: Keep your right hip in external rotation and aligned above the right knee. Engage your core to support your lower back.
- **Torso**: Lean the right side of your torso to the back of the mat, lengthening through the left side. Avoid collapsing into the lower back or back bending.
- **Arms**: Reach your right arm up towards the sky and extend through the fingertips. Gently rest your left hand on your left leg.
- **Hands**: Spin the right palm toward the back of the mat. Keep your left hand light on your left leg, avoiding putting weight on it.
- **Gaze (Drishti)**: Look up towards your lifted hand.

Contraindications and Risks
- **Neck Problems**: Proceed with caution and consider keeping your gaze down to avoid strain on your neck.
- **Specific Medical Needs**: Contraindicated for students with high blood pressure.

Side Angle Pose | Parsvakonasana

parsh-vah-koh-nah-sah-nah

Starting Position
Begin in Virabhadrasana II (Warrior II).
Lower your right forearm to your right thigh.
Sweep your left arm up to the sky.

Proper Alignment
- **Feet**: Maintain the alignment of Warrior II, grounding down through both feet.
- **Legs**: Keep your right knee bent to a 90-degree angle, spiraling your right outer thigh down, and keeping your left leg straight and active.
- **Hips**: Keep your right hip in external rotation and aligned above the right knee. Engage your core to support your lower back.
- **Torso**: Bring the right side of your torso over your right thigh. Lengthen through both sides of the waist. Engage your abdominal muscles activating Uddiyana Bandha. Ensure the spine is long, avoiding collapsing into the front leg. Slightly revolve the chest and core toward the sky as the top ribs roll back and the bottom ribs roll under.
- **Arms**: Place your right forearm lightly on your right thigh or rest your fingertips on the floor, inside or outside of the right foot. Extend your left arm up to the sky, stacking both shoulders above each other.

171

- **Head**: Ensure you have space between your ear and shoulders; refrain from tilting your head.
- **Gaze (Drishti)**: Look up towards your lifted hand, keeping your neck long and neutral.

Modifications
- **Use Props**: Modify by placing a block under the right hand, inside or outside of the foot.

Contraindications and Risks
- **Neck Pain**: Gaze directly ahead or down to maintain ease in the neck.
- **Specific Medical Needs**: Contraindicated for students with high blood pressure.
- **Knee Pain**: Avoid dumping your weight on your front leg. Keep the back leg active.

Extended Side Angle Pose | Utthita Parsvakonasana

oot-thee-tuh parsh-vuh-koh-nah-sah-nah

Starting Position
Begin in Side Angle Pose | Parsvakonasana.
Sweep your left arm up and over the head toward the front of the mat with the palm facing down.

Bound Side Angle Pose | Baddha Parsvakonasana
bah-dhuh parsh-vuh-koh-nah-sah-nah

Starting Position
Begin in Side Angle Pose | Parsvakonasana.
Extend the left arm up, spin the palm to face behind and wrap the arm behind your back.
Thread your right arm under the right thigh.
Grab the left wrist with the right hand for a bind.

Modifications
- **Using Props**: You may use a strap to help make a bind.

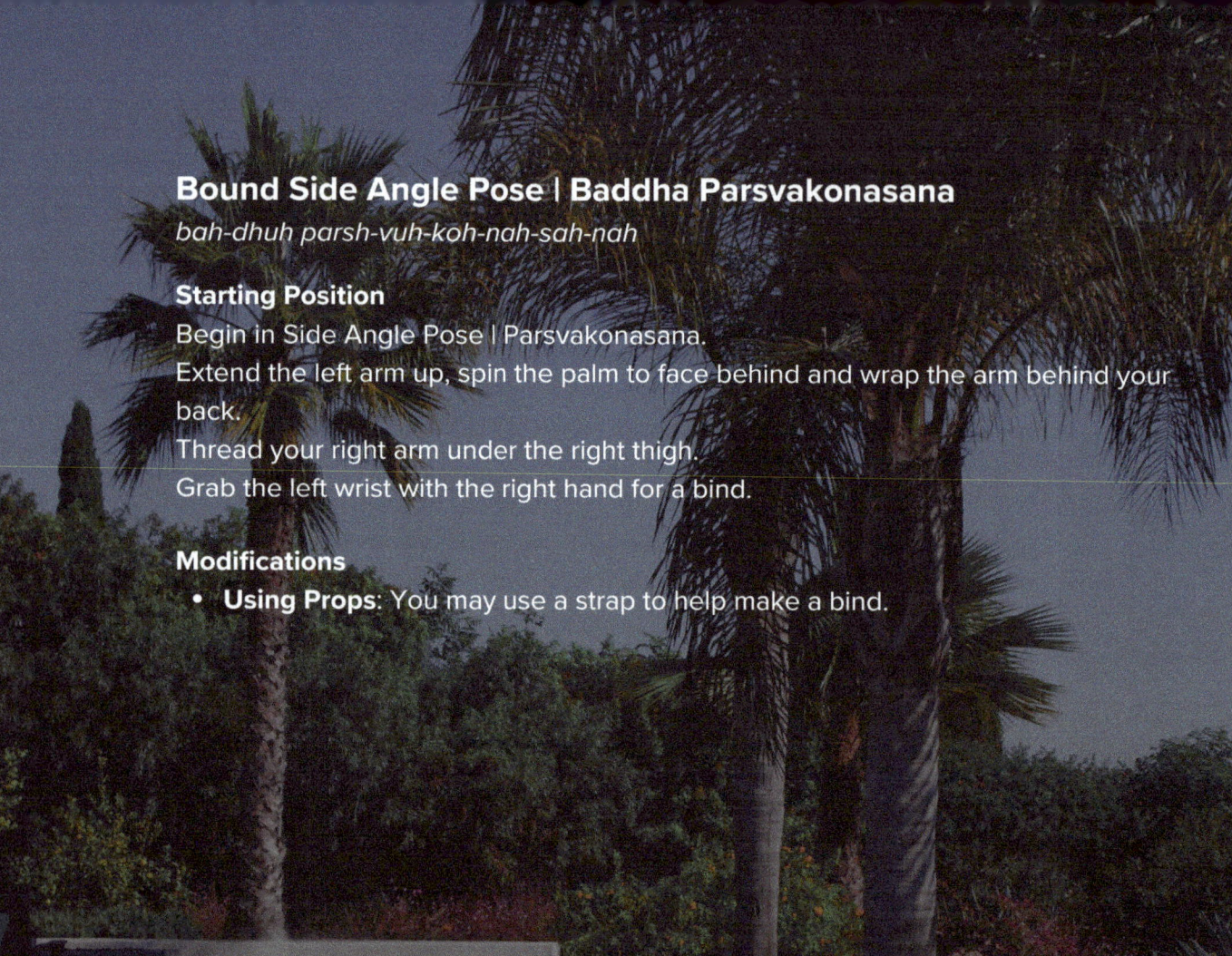

Bird of Paradise | Svarga Dvijasana

svar-guh dvee-jah-sah-nah

Starting Position
Begin in Baddha Parsvakonasana (Bound Side Angle Pose) with your right foot forward.
Shift your weight onto your right foot.
Slowly lift your left foot off the ground and step it to the top of the mat.

Proper Alignment
- **Feet**: Shift your weight onto your left heel and lift your right foot off your mat.
- **Legs**: Continue hugging your right knee toward your side ribs and lift the leg from under the thigh using your bound arms. Begin to stand on your left leg while lifting your chest.
- **Hips**: Point your two frontal hip bones straight ahead and keep your waistline in an even line.
- **Torso**: Lift the sternum upward to stand tall while drawing your tailbone down, activating Mula Bandha. Engage your core, activating Uddiyana Bandha.
- **Shoulders**: Open through your collarbones and relax your shoulders back.
- **Arms**: Maintain the bind, keeping your hands clasped or holding onto a strap.
- **Gaze (Drishti)**: Look forward to keep your neck long and neutral.

Modifications
- **Using Props**: If you have tight shoulders, you can use a strap between the hands to create additional space in your shoulders.

Contraindications and Risks
- **Specific Medical Needs**: Contraindicated for students with high blood pressure.

Tree Pose | Vrksasana
vrik-shah-sah-nah

Starting Position
Begin in Tadasana (Mountain Pose).
Shift your weight onto your right foot.
Lift the sole of your left foot and place it onto your right inner thigh.

Proper Alignment
- **Feet**: Ground down through your right foot, pressing evenly through all four corners. Root the outer edge of the right foot into the floor and lift through the inner arch to firm the thigh. Place the left foot against the right inner thigh, and hug the foot and inner thigh muscles towards each other.
- **Legs**: Engage the quadriceps of the left leg.
- **Hips**: Lengthen the sit bones toward the floor for a long lower back, activating Mula Bandha.
- **Torso**: Draw your front ribs down and draw the lower belly in to activate Uddiyana Bandha. Lift both sides of the waist evenly.
- **Arms**: Sweep your arms overhead and separate them shoulder-distance or wider.
- **Shoulders**: Slide your shoulders down the back and keep the neck long.
- **Hands**: Palms can face each other or you can bring the index and thumb together for Gyan Mudra to enhance stability.
- **Gaze (Drishti)**: Keep a focused gaze at eye level to maintain balance.

Modifications
- **Hands to Prayer**: Modify by bringing your hands to Anjali Mudra for more stability and balance.
- **Wall Support**: Students with Vertigo or Osteoporosis may try this pose near a wall for support.
- **Alternating Pose**: Students with trouble balancing or leg weakness may modify this pose by placing their foot below their knee or resting their toes on the floor. Your lifted foot must always rest above or below the knee of your standing leg. Putting pressure on your knee could cause injury to your standing leg.

Contraindications and Risks
- **Knee Issues**: Contraindicated for students with knee injuries. Proceed with caution and consider modification.

Triangle Pose | Trikonasana

tree-koh-nah-sah-nah

Starting Position

- Begin from Virabhadrasana II (Warrior II) with your right foot forward.
- Straighten your right leg and slightly shorten the distance between your feet by drawing the left foot forward.
- Keep your left foot on a gentle angle, with your left toes pointing slightly to the front corner of the mat.

Proper Alignment

- **Feet**: Point your right toes directly ahead. Seal the outer edge of your left foot into the floor, pointing the toes slightly inward and heel slightly outward.
- **Legs**: Engage your right thigh by drawing the kneecap up. Firm your inner thighs toward the midline, engaging the adductors.
- **Hips**: Externally rotate the right hip by spiraling its outer side underneath and in. Internally rotate the left hip.
- **Torso**: Draw your front ribs down to prevent a backbend while drawing the abdominals in and reaching the center of your sternum forward.

- **Arms**: Extend your left arm up to create a straight line of energy to the fingertips of the right arm.
- **Shoulders**: Rotate your chest open and stack your shoulders directly on top of each other.
- **Hands**: Place your right hand lightly on your shin, ankle, the floor, or on a block. Extend your left hand up towards the sky.
- **Gaze (Drishti)**: Look up towards your left thumb.

Modifications
- **Using Props**: To support the pose, place your right hand on a block inside or outside your right foot.
- **Neck Issues**: Gaze ahead or down towards the ground to avoid strain on your neck.

Contraindications and Risks
- **Specific Medical Needs**: Contraindicated for students with low blood pressure.

Extended Triangle Pose | Utthita Trikonasana
oot-thee-tuh tree-koh-nah-sah-nah

Starting Position
Begin in Triangle Pose (Trikonasana).
Extend your top arm over the head towards the front of the room with the palm facing down.

Half Moon Pose | Ardha Chandrasana
ard-ha chan-drah-sah-nah

Starting Position

Begin in Triangle Pose (Trikonasana).

Place your right fingertips about a foot ahead of your right foot on the floor or preferably a yoga block.

Shift your weight forward onto your right foot and lift your left leg parallel to the floor using abdominal muscles.

Proper Alignment

- **Feet:** With the right toes pointing straight ahead like arrows, ground down through your right foot. Lift your left leg parallel to the floor using abdominal muscles. Flex the toes of the left foot with the arch parallel to the floor and the big toe pointing slightly down. Keep your energy extending through your left heel as the leg muscles are active.

- **Legs:** Keep your right knee facing directly ahead over the center of your foot. Welcome a micro-bend in the knee of your standing leg to maintain stability. Slightly draw your left leg a few inches ahead of your hip bone to avoid back bending.

181

- **Hips**: Externally rotate your right standing hip, stacking your left lifted hip over your right.
- **Torso**: Lengthen through your spine, extending sideways over your standing right leg. Avoid collapsing into your side. Continue to engage your abdominals to lengthen your tailbone toward the back of your mat while drawing the front ribs down to prevent a backbend. Open your chest and belly button to the side and avoid rotating downward.
- **Arms**: Extend your right hand down towards the floor or a block. Reach your left arm up towards the sky.
- **Shoulders**: Keep opening the left shoulder to the side of the mat. Draw both shoulders down the back, away from the ear, by wrapping the triceps back. Draw your shoulder blades apart and spread the collarbones to open up the front of the body.
- **Head**: Notice that there is one straight line of energy from the crown of your head to your extended heel.
- **Gaze (Drishti)**: Look up towards your left hand. Option to look to the side or down at your front foot if your neck is sensitive.

Modifications
- **Using Props**: Rest your hand on a block a few inches ahead of your standing foot, to find balance in this pose.
- **Wall Support**: Beginners may modify this pose by standing against a wall for support.

Contraindications and Risks
- **Neck Issues**: Keep your gaze down towards the ground to avoid strain on your neck.

Bound Half Moon Pose |
Ardha Chandra Chapasana
ard-ha chan-drah chah-pah-sah-nah

Starting Position
Begin in Half Moon Pose (Ardha Chandrasana).
Bend your lifted left knee.
Reach your back hand with your left hand to grasp the lifted left foot.
Hug the heel toward the glute, keeping your left quadriceps facing the side.

182

Hand to Big Toe Pose II | Utthita Hasta Padangusthasana II

oot-thee-tuh hah-stuh pah-dahng-goosh-tah-sah-nah

Starting Position

Beginning in Utthita Hasta Padangusthasana I (Hand to Big Toe Pose I) with your right leg lifted, open your right leg toward the side, sending energy out through your heel. Place your left hand on the hip of your standing leg.

Proper Alignment

- **Feet**: Ground down through your left foot, pressing evenly through all four corners.
- **Legs**: Keep the right femur descending toward the mat. Keep your left foot and knee pointing directly ahead to maintain the health and safety of your knee.
- **Hips**: Square your left hip forward in a neutral rotation, and externally rotate the right hip as you plug it into the hip socket. Keep both sides of your waist even.
- **Torso**: Lengthen through your spine, lifting through the crown of your head. Engage your abdominal muscles and lift the low pelvic floor, activating Uddiyana Bandha and Mula Bandha to support your lower back.

- **Arms**: Extend your right arm out to the side at shoulder height for balance. Hold your right big toe with your two peace fingers, keeping your arm straight.
- **Head**: Keep your chin parallel to the floor. Elongate both sides of your neck.
- **Gaze (Drishti)**: Gaze away from the lifted leg and to the left side.

Modifications
- **Wall Support**: Students may modify this pose by standing against a wall for support.
- **Alternating Pose**: Students with lower back pain or dizziness can perform this pose by reclining on the floor.

Contraindications and Risks
- **Shoulder Injury**: Students with shoulder injuries can use a strap on the lifted leg.

Temple Pose | Stupa
stoo-puh

Starting Position
Begin in Tadasana (Mountain Pose).
Step your feet wide apart.
Turn your toes out slightly and your heels in.

Proper Alignment
- **Feet**: Ground down through your feet, pressing evenly through all four corners. Keep your toes turned out slightly while keeping your weight in your heels.
- **Legs**: Bend your knees 90 degrees, lowering your hips towards the earth. Keep your knees aligned with your ankles.
- **Hips**: Sit your hips back and down as if sitting into a chair. Lift your low pelvic floor, activating Mula Bandha to support your lower back.
- **Torso**: Lengthen the lower back toward the floor, lifting your lower belly and drawing the front ribs down, activating Uddiyana Bandha to prevent a backbend.

185

- **Shoulders**: Keep your shoulders relaxed and your chest lifted.
- **Arms**: Extend your arms up to the sky at shoulder-distance or bend your elbows and bring your hands to prayer position, Anjali Mudra, to the center of your chest.
- **Head**: Lifting through the crown of your head, keeping your neck long and neutral.
- **Gaze (Drishti):** Look forward.

Modifications

- **Adjust Stance**: Keep your feet closer and bend your knees less deeply to reduce strain.

Contraindications and Risks

- **Knee Issues**: Contraindicated for students with knee injuries or instability.

Inversions and Arm Balances

Inversions involve poses where the head is positioned below the heart, while arm balances require balancing the body weight on the hands and arms.

All alignment instructions provided in this book are for the right side. In yoga practice, we often start with the right side, which is a tradition in many yoga classes. However, it is essential to consistently perform these poses on both sides to maintain balance in the body.

After completing the pose on the right side, please ensure you repeat the same pose on the left side, following the exact alignment. Practicing on both sides will help you achieve a well-rounded and balanced practice, promoting symmetry and strength in your body.

Downward Facing Dog | Adho Mukha Svanasana

ah-doh moo-khuh shvah-nah-sah-nah

Starting Position

Begin from Bhujangasana (Cobra) or Urdhva Mukha Svanasana (Upward Facing Dog).
Tuck your toes.
Lift your hips up and back and drop your head down between your biceps.

Proper Alignment

- **Feet**: Place your feet hip-width apart, hiding the heels behind the toes to keep them in a neutral rotation. Spread your toes and allow your heels to gravitate toward the earth.
- **Legs**: Straighten your legs and engage your quadriceps. Keep a slight bend in your knees if your hamstrings are tight. Hug the inner thigh muscles in toward each other.
- **Hips**: Lift your hips upwards, elongating your spine. Imagine creating space between each vertebra. Tilt your pelvic bowl toward your face to lengthen the sacrum.
- **Torso**: Draw your belly in and engage your abdominal muscles, activating Uddiyana Bandha. Lengthen through your side waist and extend your spine.
- **Shoulders**: Slide the shoulders (trapezius muscles) away from your ears and lift them toward the hips.

189

- **Arms**: Straighten your arms, externally rotate your upper arms outward, and hollow your armpits to broaden your shoulders. Allow the eyes of the elbows to face each other as you hug the arms in towards each other.
- **Hands**: Separate the hands shoulder-distance apart or wider to open across the chest. Press your hands firmly into the mat, spreading your fingers wide. Keep your wrists aligned with your shoulders, with the wrist line straight. Press evenly through all corners of the palms and fingertips, activating Hasta Bandha, the slight suction cup in the palms.
- **Head**: Align your ears between your upper arms, and keep the space between your shoulders and ears long and spacious.
- **Gaze (Drishti)**: Rest your gaze comfortably down and back at your feet or towards your navel, keeping your neck long and relaxed.

Modifications
- **Slight Bend**: Keep a slight bend in your knees to reduce strain on your hamstrings.
- **Wall Support**: If you have wrist pain or carpal tunnel syndrome, modify the pose by placing your hands on yoga blocks or a wall instead of the mat for less pressure.
- **Alternative Pose:** To ease tension from your wrists, place your forearms on the mat, coming into Dolphin Pose as a modification.
- **Using Props**: You can support your head with a block or place two blocks underneath your hands.

Contraindications and Risks
- **Pregnancy**: Contraindicated for students in the late stages of pregnancy.

Side Plank | Vasisthasana

vah-sisht-hah-sah-nah

Starting Position

Begin in Plank Pose (Phalakasana).
Shift your weight onto your right hand and the outer edge of your right foot.
Extend your left arm towards the sky.

Proper Alignment

- **Feet**: Bring the inner edges of your feet together at the back of the mat and spin to the outside edge of your right foot, stacking your left foot directly on top, with the inner edges of the feet touching.
- **Legs**: Lift your quadriceps muscles away from the knees and hug your inner thigh muscles toward each other to keep your legs strong and active.
- **Hips**: Lengthen your tailbone towards your heels, creating a straight line from head to heels. Stack your left hip directly above the right hip and slightly warp the top left hip forward, ensuring the pose does not become a backbend. Engage your abdominal muscles and lift the low pelvic floor, activating Uddiyana Bandha and Mula Bandha to support your lower back.

191

- **Torso**: Draw your front ribs down and your belly toward your spine, keeping a micro crunch in your core.
- **Arms**: Extend your left arm up towards the sky, creating a straight line from your two hands.
- **Shoulders**: Slide the trapezius down the back, draw the shoulder blades away from the midline of the body, while reaching the arms away from each other, and actively press the floor away.
- **Hands**: Stack your right wrist directly under your right shoulder. Press your right hand firmly into the mat, spreading your fingers wide. Reach through the left fingertips towards the sky.
- **Gaze (Drishti)**: Look up towards your left thumb or forward to maintain balance.

Modifications
- **Knee Support**: For additional stability, especially for students with wrist, shoulder, or elbow pain, you can place their bottom knee onto the mat directly under their bottom hip or by resting the bottom forearm on the mat. Or cross the top ankle in front of the bottom ankle.
- **Shoulder Support**: Lower on your right forearm.

Contraindications and Risks
- **Wrist Issues:** This pose is contraindicated for students with carpal tunnel syndrome or other wrist injuries.

Dolphin Pose

Starting Position
Begin from Forearm Plank.
Tuck your toes.
Lift your hips up and back, and walk your feet closer to your arms until the shoulders stack directly above the elbows.

Proper Alignment
- **Feet**: Place your feet hip-width apart, staying on the balls of the feet. Walk your feet forward towards your elbows to shorten your stance. Descend your heels towards the mat.
- **Legs**: Straighten your legs and engage your quadriceps. Keep a slight bend in your knees if your hamstrings are tight.
- **Hips**: Lift your hips high, lengthening your spine. Imagine creating space between each vertebra.
- **Torso**: Draw your belly in and engage your core, activating Uddiyana Bandha. Lengthen through your sides and extend your spine.
- **Arms**: Parallel your forearms with each other. Separate the elbows shoulder-distance apart, creating a 90-degree angle. Press your forearms firmly into the mat, spreading your fingers wide. Rotate your upper arms outward to broaden your shoulders.

- **Shoulders**: Stack the shoulders directly above the elbows, creating a straight line from the shoulder to the elbow. Slide the trapezius muscles away from the ears, keeping your neck long.
- **Hands**: Keep your wrists aligned with your elbows. Rest your palms flat on the earth and spread your fingers wide as you press down.
- **Gaze (Drishti)**: Look between your feet or towards your navel, keeping your neck long and relaxed.

Modifications
- **Using Props**: If your elbows splay wider than your shoulders, use a strap around your upper arms to keep your elbows shoulder-width apart.
- **Shoulder and Neck Issues**: Students with tight shoulders should proceed cautiously.

Plow Pose I Halasana

hah-lah-sah-nah

Starting Position
Begin in Legs up the Wall (Viparita Karani).
Extend your legs up and over your head.
Bring your toes towards the floor behind your head.

Proper Alignment
- **Feet**: Keep your feet together and pointed, or flex your feet and press your toes into the floor.
- **Legs**: Keep your legs straight and active, firming your quadriceps and inner thighs.
- **Hips**: Lift your hips up, lengthening through your spine. Engage your core to support your lower back. Stack your hips directly over your shoulders.
- **Torso**: Lengthen through your spine, extending through the crown of your head.
- **Arms**: Extend your arms down the mat, pressing your palms into the floor. Alternatively, interlace your fingers and press your arms into the mat.

- **Shoulders**: Draw your shoulder blades toward each other, keeping the neck long and maintaining the cervical spine's natural curve.
- **Neck**: Keep the neck safe by allowing enough space between your chin and your chest so that the breath can flow freely through your throat.
- **Head**: Carefully rest the back of your head on the floor. Keep most of your weight onto the shoulders to alleviate pressure from your head and neck.
- **Hands**: Press your palms or interlace your fingers, grounding your arms into the mat.
- **Gaze (Drishti)**: Keep your gaze towards your navel, avoiding neck movement.

Modifications

- **Using Props**: Place a small folded blanket under the back of the neck for support.

Contraindications and Risks

- **Specific Medical Needs**: This pose is contraindicated for students with high blood pressure, a history of stroke, hernia, and acid reflux.
- **Neck Pain**: Proceed with caution, or stay in Supported Shoulder Stand (Salamba Sarvangasana) or Legs up the Wall (Viparita Karani), if there is no wall, keep the legs up in the air.

Shoulderstand I Sarvangasana

sar-van-gah-sah-nah

Starting Position
Begin in Legs up the Wall (Viparita Karani).
Lift your hips towards the sky and stack them over your shoulders.
Place your hands on your lower back.

Proper Alignment
- **Feet**: Keep your feet together and pointed, or flex your feet towards the sky. Reach upward through the toes.
- **Legs**: Keep your legs straight and active, engaging your quadriceps and inner thighs.
- **Hips**: Lift your hips upward, stacking them directly over your shoulders. Engage your core to support your lower back.
- **Torso**: Lengthen through your spine.
- **Arms**: Press your upper arms to the mat and your hands into your back for support to relieve any tension in your neck. Hug the elbows in toward each other, keeping their shoulder-distance apart.
- **Neck**: Keep the neck safe by allowing enough space between your chin and your chest so that the breath can flow freely through your throat.
- **Head**: Carefully rest the back of your head on the floor. Keeping most of your weight onto the shoulders, alleviating pressure off your head and neck.
- **Gaze (Drishti)**: Keep your gaze towards your navel, avoiding neck movement.

Modifications
- **Neck Support**: To protect your neck and maintain the curve of your cervical spine, place a rolled blanket underneath the back of your neck.

Contraindications and Risks
- **Specific Medical Needs**: Contraindicated for students with a history of stroke, hernia, or acid reflux.
- **Neck Pain**: Proceed with caution or stay in Legs up the Wall (Viparita Karani). If there is no wall, keep the legs up in the air. You can also stay in Supported Bridge Pose (Salamba Setu Bandha Sarvangasana).

Shoulderstand Exit | Karnapidasana

car-nuh-pee-dah-sah-nah

Starting Position

Begin in Sarvangasana (Shoulder Stand).
Separate the legs wide apart and bend your knees.
Drape your knees by your ears.

Proper Alignment

- **Feet**: With the feet wide apart, rest the tops of the feet on the floor.
- **Legs**: Bend your knees and bring them towards your ears. Rest your knees, shins, and tops of your feet on the floor.
- **Hips**: Lift your hips upwards toward the sky. Lengthen through your sacrum, slightly rounding the spine.
- **Torso**: Slightly pull the navel in to support your lower back.
- **Arms**: Extend your arms along the mat, pressing your palms into the floor.
- **Hands**: Press your palms flat on the mat, grounding your arms down into the earth.
- **Gaze (Drishti):** Keep an upward gaze, avoiding neck movement.

Contraindications and Risks

- **Neck Issues**: Contraindicated for students with neck injuries. Avoid any movement of the neck, and keep your gaze fixed.
- **Shoulder Injuries:** Contraindicated for students with shoulder injuries.

201

Headstand A | Sirsasana A

sheer-shah-sah-nah

Starting Position

Begin in a tabletop position on the hands and knees.

Interlace your fingers, hiding the last pinky inside of the opposite palm.

Rest the crown of your head on the mat and the back of your head in your two cupped hands.

Proper Alignment

- **Hands:** Interlace your fingers, creating a cup for the back of your head. Feel the connection and support in your hands.
- **Shoulders:** Draw your shoulder blades (trapezius muscles) away from your ears, keeping your neck long.
- **Arms:** Hug the elbows toward each other, keeping the elbows shoulder-distance apart. Press your forearms firmly into the mat, creating a stable base.
- **Torso:** Hug the lower ribcage inward and pull the navel in, keeping a micro crunch in your core. Engage your abdominal muscles and lift the low pelvic floor, activating Uddiyana Bandha and Mula Bandha. Lengthen through your spine. Feel the elongation and openness in your torso.
- **Feet:** Tuck your toes under and lift your hips up toward the sky. Walk your feet closer to your arms until the hips stack on top of the shoulders.
- **Hips:** Lift your hips high, stacking them directly over your shoulders.
- **Legs:** Float one leg up at a time, bringing both legs towards the sky. Stack the legs directly above the hips and shoulders. Straighten your legs and engage your quadriceps. Reach through the balls of your feet and spread your toes.

Modifications

- **Wall Support**: Practice near a wall for added support and stability.
- **Shoulder Strength**: Avoid placing weight on your neck and head. Students can have the option to keep their feet on the ground and focus on building shoulder strength in Dolphin Pose.

Contraindications and Risks

- **Specific Medical Needs**: Contraindicated for students with a history of **neck issues**, **shoulder pain**, **high blood pressure**, **heart disease**, **stroke**, or **acid reflux**.

Headstand B I Sirsasana B

sheer-shah-sah-nah

Starting Position

Begin in a tabletop position on the hands and knees.

Place the crown of your head on the mat

Hug the elbows in toward the ribcage and bend them into a 90-degree angle.

Proper Alignment

- **Hands:** Plant the palms of your hands flat on the floor, with the fingertips pointing toward your face. Stack the wrists directly underneath the elbows, creating a tripod base with your head.
- **Shoulders:** Draw your shoulder blades (trapezius muscles) away from your ears, keeping your neck long.
- **Arms:** Hug the elbows in toward each other, keeping the elbows shoulder-distance apart. Keep the upper arms parallel with the earth. Stack the elbows directly above the wrists to create a 90-degree angle.
- **Torso:** Hug the lower ribcage inward and pull the navel in, keeping a micro crunch in your core. Engage your abdominal muscles and lift the low pelvic floor, activating Uddiyana Bandha and Mula Bandha. Lengthen through your spine. Feel the elongation and openness in your torso.
- **Feet:** Tuck your toes under and lift your hips up toward the sky. Walk your feet closer to your arms until the hips stack on top of the shoulders.
- **Hips:** Lift your hips high, stacking them directly over your shoulders.
- **Legs:** Float one leg up at a time, bringing both legs towards the sky. Stack the legs directly above the hips and shoulders. Straighten your legs and engage your quadriceps. Reach through the balls of your feet and spread your toes.

Modifications

- **Wall Support**: Practice near a wall for added support and stability.
- **Shoulder Strength**: Rest your knees on your elbows and bring the big toes together for a tripod position or keep your feet on the ground.

Contraindications and Risks

- **Specific Medical Needs:** Contraindicated for students with a history of **neck issues, shoulder pain, high blood pressure, heart disease, stroke,** or **acid reflux.**

Handstand | Adho Mukha Vrksasana

ah-doh moo-khuh vrik-shah-sah-nah

Starting Position

Begin in Downward Facing Dog (Adho Mukha Svanasana).

Walk your feet closer to your hands and hollow your upper body into a micro cow pose.

Look between your hands or slightly forward.

Lift one leg up directly above the hips and head, bringing both legs towards the sky.

Proper Alignment

- **Hands**: Push the floor away from you, pressing evenly through all four corners, activating Hasta Bandha.
- **Shoulders**: Draw your shoulder blades (trapezius muscles) away from your ears, keeping your neck long.
- **Arms**: Wrap the elbows in toward each other, keeping the eyes of the elbows facing each other. Keep your elbows straight.
- **Torso**: Hug the lower ribcage inward and pull the navel in, keeping a micro crunch in your core. Engage your abdominal muscles and lift the low pelvic floor, activating Uddiyana Bandha and Mula Bandha. Lengthen through your spine. Feel the elongation and openness in your torso. There should be a straight line from head to toe.
- **Hips**: Stack your hips directly over your shoulders.
- **Legs**: Float one leg up at a time, bringing both legs towards the sky. Stack the legs directly above the hips and shoulders. Straighten your legs and engage your quadriceps. Reach through the balls of your feet and spread your toes.
- **Feet**: Lift one foot at a time towards the sky, reaching through the ball of your foot.

Modifications

- **Wall Support**: Practice near a wall for added support and stability.
- Using Props: Students may use a strap above the elbows to practice proper alignment and engagement of the arms.
- **Alternative Pose:** Focus on building shoulder strength in Dolphin Pose or Forearm Balance before attempting Handstand.

Contraindications and Risks

- **Specific Medical Needs**: Contraindicated for students with high blood pressure, glaucoma, or a history of stroke. Contraindications for students with shoulder and elbow injuries.

Forearm Balance I Pincha Mayurasana

peen-cha my-yoor-ah-sah-nah

Starting Position
Begin in Dolphin Pose.

Tuck your toes under and lift your hips up toward the sky.

Walk your feet closer to your arms until the hips stack on top of the shoulders.

Look between the hands.

Proper Alignment
- **Hands**: Plant the palms of your hands flat on the floor, with the fingertips pointing away from your face. Keep the hands elbow-distance apart and elbows shoulder-width apart, creating a 90-degree angle in the elbows.
- **Head**: Keep your head elevated off the mat, avoiding neck movement.
- **Shoulders**: Draw your shoulder blades (trapezius muscles) away from your ears. Drive through the shoulders to lift your body off the ground and upward toward the sky.
- **Arms**: Wrap the elbows in toward the midline of the body, keeping the elbows shoulder-distance apart. Rest your forearms on the mat parallel to each other and shoulder-width apart.
- **Torso**: Hug the lower ribcage inward and pull the navel in, keeping a micro crunch in your core. Engage your abdominal muscles and lift the low pelvic floor, activating Uddiyana Bandha and Mula Bandha. Lengthen through your spine. Feel the elongation and openness in your torso.
- **Hips**: Lift your hips high, stacking them directly over your shoulders.
- **Legs**: Float one leg at a time, bringing both legs towards the sky. Stack the legs directly above the hips and shoulders. Straighten your legs and engage your quadriceps. Reach through the balls of your feet and spread your toes.
- **Feet**: Tuck your toes under and lift your hips up toward the sky. Walk your feet closer to your arms until the hips stack on top of the shoulders.

Modifications
- **Balance**: Practice near a wall for added support and stability.
- **Alternative Pose:** Focus on building shoulder strength in Dolphin Pose before attempting Forearm Balance.

Contraindications and Risks
- **Specific Medical Needs**: Contraindicated for students with a history of stroke, high blood pressure, or glaucoma.
- **Shoulder Injuries**: Contraindicated for students with shoulder injuries.

Scorpion I Vrschikasana

vrish-chee-kah-sah-nah

Starting Position

Begin in Pincha Mayurasana (Forearm Balance).

Bend your knees to bring your feet towards the back of your head.

Option to interlace the fingers.

Modifications

- **Balance**: Practice near a wall for added support and stability.
- **Alternative Pose:** Focus on building shoulder strength in Dolphin Pose before attempting Forearm Balance.

Contraindications and Risks

- **Specific Medical Needs**: Contraindicated for students with a history of stroke, high blood pressure, or glaucoma.
- **Shoulder Injuries**: Contraindicated for students with shoulder injuries.

Crow Pose | Bakasana

bah-kuh-sah-nah

Starting Position

Begin in a Yogi Squat (Malasana).
Lift your hips and shift your weight forward.
Place your knees onto your upper arms.

Proper Alignment

- **Gaze (Drishti)**: Look slightly forward.
- **Hands**: Ground down through your palms, pressing evenly through all four corners, activating Hasta Bandha.
- **Arms**: Hug the elbows toward the ribcage. Bend your elbows slightly, spinning the eyes of the elbows toward the front of the mat. When ready, begin to press your arms straight.
- **Torso**: Shift your weight forward and hug the lower ribcage inward. Pull the navel in, like in a cow pose. Engage your abdominal muscles and lift the low pelvic floor, activating Uddiyana Bandha and Mula Bandha.

- **Hips**: Lift your hips upward toward the sky.
- **Legs**: Bend your knees and place them onto your upper arms, engaging your inner thighs.
- **Feet**: Lift your feet off the mat and bring the big toes together.

Modifications
- **Using Props**: Place a block under your feet for added support.
- **Wrist Issues**: Avoid putting too much weight on your wrists
- **New to Balancing**: Students new to arm balances may modify the pose by placing their toes on blocks to explore shifting their weight forward with support.

Contraindications and Risks
- **Specific Medical Needs**: Contraindicated for pregnant students with high blood pressure.

Side Crow | Parsva Bakasana

parsh-vuh bah-kuh-sah-nah

Starting Position

Begin in a Utkatasana (Chair Pose).

Shift the weight toward the toes and lift the heels.

Bring your hands to your heart and twist your torso to the right, bringing your left elbow to the outside of your right knee, arriving at a twisting chair pose.

Proper Alignment

- **Hands**: Plant Your palms along the side edge of your mat shoulder-distance apart, pressing evenly through all four corners.
- **Gaze (Drishti)**: look between your hands and slightly forwards
- **Arms**: Bend your elbows at a 90° angle and hug the elbows inward toward each other, keeping them shoulder-distance apart. Align your biceps so that they are parallel to the floor. Stack your elbows directly above your wrists.
- **Torso**: Twist your torso to the right. Engage your abdominal muscles and lift the low pelvic floor, activating Uddiyana Bandha and Mula Bandha.
- **Hips**: Stack the hips on top of each other, coming into a twisting position.
- **Legs**: Bend your knees at a 90° angle and rest the right thigh on the left upper arm. Engage the inner thigh muscles. Stack the shins on top of each other and align them parallel with the earth, keeping them at hip height.
- **Feet**: Lift your heels and bring your toes together.

Modifications

- **Using Props**: Place blocks underneath your shoulder at the highest height for support.
- **Wrist Issues**: Avoid putting too much weight on your wrists.
- **Shoulder Injuries**: Avoid putting too much weight on your shoulders. Focus on building strength gradually.

Contraindications and Risks

- **Specific Medical Needs**: Contraindicated for pregnant students with high blood pressure.

213

Fallen Angel | Devaduuta Panna Asana

day-vuh-doo-tuh pah-nuh ah-sah-nah

Starting Position

Begin in Parsva Bakasana (Side Crow) with your right side down.

Gently lower your right temple toward the earth.

Reach your left leg toward the ceiling and send energy out through the balls of your foot as your toes spread.

Modifications

- **Using Props**: Place blocks underneath your shoulder at the highest height for support.
- **Wrist Issues**: Avoid putting too much weight on your wrists.
- **Shoulder Injuries**: Avoid putting too much weight on your shoulders. Focus on building strength gradually.
- **Neck:** Avoid putting too much pressure on your head to protect your neck. Send your weight back into your hips, core, and legs.

Contraindications and Risks

- **Specific Medical Needs:** Contraindicated for pregnant students with high blood pressure.

214

Flying Pigeon I Eka Pada Galavasana

eh-kuh pah-duh guh-lah-vuh-sah-nah

Starting Position

Begin in Standing Pigeon Pose (Utthita Eka Pada Rajakapotasana).
Balancing on your right leg, plant your hands shoulder-distance apart, and rest your left shin on your triceps. Lift the right leg off the mat and send it toward the back. Point the back right toes.

Proper Alignment

- **Gaze (Drishti)**: Look slightly forward between your hands.
- **Hands**: Keep your hands shoulder-distance apart. Spread your fingers wide, ground down through your palms, pressing evenly through all four corners, activating Hasta Bandha. Point your fingertips directly ahead.
- **Arms**: Bend your elbows at a 90° angle so your biceps are parallel with the earth. Stack your elbows directly above your wrists. Wrap the elbows inward towards the rib cage.
- **Torso**: Hug the rib cage inward towards the spine, keeping a micro crunch in your core. Engage your abdominal muscles and lift the low pelvic floor, activating Uddiyana Bandha and Mula Bandha.
- **Hips**: Externally rotate your left hip to draw the left knee toward the earth.
- **Legs**: Keep the left knee bent and your left shin parallel to the front line of your mat.
- **Feet**: Flex your left foot to protect your knee.

Modifications

- **Using Props**: Place a block under your left foot for added support.

Contraindications and Risks

- **Pregnancy**: Contraindicated for students who are pregnant. Students are advised to proceed with caution.

Pose Dedicated to the Sage Koundinya I | Eka Pada Koundinynsana I

eh-kuh pah-duh koon-deen-yah-sah-nah

Starting Position

Begin in Parsva Bakasana (Side Crow Pose) with your knees stacked on the outer edge of your upper left arm.
Extend your right leg straight out to the side, parallel to the front of your mat, and flex the foot. Extend your left leg straight back, at hip height. Flex your left foot and press through the heel. Engage the quadriceps and inner thigh muscles to keep the legs lifted and active.

Modifications

- **Alternative Pose:** Focus on building shoulder strength in Plank Pose before attempting Koundinyasana I.
- **Wrist Issues**: Avoid putting too much weight on your wrists. Modify with a folded mat or towel under your wrists.

Contraindications and Risks

- Contraindicated for students with shoulders, elbows, and wrist injuries.

Pose Dedicated to the Sage Koundinya II | Eka Pada Koundinyasana II

eh-kuh pah-duh koon-deen-yah-sah-nah

Starting Position

Begin in Adho Mukha Svanasana (Downward Facing Dog).
Lift the right leg up to three-legged dog.
Bring your right knee to your upper right arm.

Proper Alignment

- **Gaze (Drishti):** Look slightly forward, keeping your neck long and neutral.
- **Hands:** Keep your hands shoulder-distance apart, pressing evenly through all four corners, cultivating Hasta Bandha.
- **Shoulders:** Keep your weight even on both shoulders. Align your shoulders with the elbows.
- **Arms:** Bend your elbows At a 90° angle so that your biceps are parallel with the Earth. Stack your elbows directly above your wrists. Wrap the elbows inward towards the rib cage.
- **Torso:** Hug the rib cage inward towards the spine, keeping a micro crunch in your core. Engage your abdominal muscles and lift the low pelvic floor, activating Uddiyana Bandha and Mula Bandha.

- **Hips:** Keep your hips at hip height.
- **Legs:** Bring the inner thigh of your right leg to the outer arm. Shift the weight forward and float the back left leg up from the floor. When ready, straighten both legs.
- **Feet:** Lift your left foot and extend your right leg out to the side, keeping the extended leg's foot flexed.

Modifications
- **Alternative Pose:** Focus on building shoulder strength in Plank Pose before attempting Koundinyasana I.
- **Wrist Issues**: Avoid putting too much weight on your wrists. Modify with a folded mat or towel under your wrists.

Contraindications and Risks
- Contraindicated for students with shoulders, elbows, and wrist injuries.

Scale Pose I Tolasana

toh-luh-sah-nah

Starting Position

Begin in Padmasana (Lotus Pose).
Place your hands on the mat beside your hips.
Press your hands firmly into the ground as you lift your hips off the mat.

Proper Alignment

- **Gaze (Drishti):** Look slightly forward, keeping your neck long and neutral.
- **Hands:** Ground down through your palms, pressing evenly through all four corners.
- **Arms:** Press your hands firmly into the mat, keeping your elbows straight and your shoulders engaged.
- **Torso:** Lengthen through your spine, extending through the crown of your head.
- **Hips:** Lift your hips off the ground. Engage your abdominal muscles and lift the low pelvic floor, activating Uddiyana Bandha and Mula Bandha.
- **Legs:** Cross your legs and engage your inner thighs.
- **Feet:** Rest the top of the feet on top of the inner thighs.

Modifications

- **Alternative Pose:** Modify the leg position if the full Lotus Pose is inaccessible. Use a cross-legged position instead.

Contraindications and Risks

- Contraindicated for students with shoulders, elbows, and wrist injuries

Shoulder Pressing Pose | Bhujapidasana

boo-jah-pee-dah-sah-nah

Starting Position

Begin in Yogi Squat (Malasana).

Plant your hands flat on the ground, separating them shoulder-distance apart or wider.

Lift your hips and place your knees on your upper arms.

Bring your feet together.

Proper Alignment

- **Gaze (Drishti):** Look down, keeping the back of your neck long and neutral.
- **Hands:** Ground down through your palms, pressing evenly through all four corners.
- **Shoulders:** Slide your right shoulder behind your right knee and slide your left shoulder behind your left knee.
- **Arms:** Bend your elbows slightly, press your hands firmly into the mat, and spread your fingers wide.
- **Torso:** Lengthen through your spine, drawing your belly in and up.
- **Hips:** Lift your hips up, engaging your core and activating Mula Bandha to support your balance.
- **Legs:** Bend your knees and bring them onto your upper arms, engaging your inner thighs.
- **Feet:** Lift your feet and cross one ankle on top of the other.

Modifications

- **Alternative Pose:** Modify the leg position if the full Lotus Pose is inaccessible. Use a cross-legged position instead.

Contraindications and Risks

- Contraindicated for students with shoulders, elbows, and wrist injuries.

Grasshopper Pose | Parsva Bhuja Dandasana

pahr-svah boo-jah dahn-dah-sah-nah

Starting Position

Begin balancing on the right leg in Standing Pigeon Pose (Utthita Eka Pada Rajakapotasana).
Bring your palms together in a prayer pose, Anjali Mudra, at your heart center.
Twist your torso to the right, and rest your left elbow inside the sole of your left foot.
Plant your hands on the long side of your mat shoulder with the part.

Proper Alignment

- **Gaze (Drishti):** Look between your fingertips and slightly forward.
- **Hands:** Press your hands firmly into the mat, spreading your fingers wide. Keep your weight even on all four corners of your hands, with a slight suction cup in the hands activating Hasta Bandha.
- **Arms:** Bend your elbows At a 90° angle so that your biceps are parallel with the Earth. Stack your elbows directly above your wrists. Wrap the elbows inward towards the rib cage.
- **Torso:** Hug the rib cage inward towards the spine, keeping a micro crunch in your core. Engage your abdominal muscles and lift the low pelvic floor, activating Uddiyana Bandha and Mula Bandha.
- **Hips:** Keep your hips at the same level and height as your shoulders, stacking one hip on top of the other in a twisting position.

- **Legs**: Lift your left knee toward your chest. Place the left knee above the left ankle. Flex the right foot and extend the outer thigh toward the floor, parallel to the front line of your mat.
- **Feet**: Keep the sole of your left foot and your left elbow connected.

Modifications
- **Alternative Pose:** Modify the pose by staying in Standing Pigeon Pose (Utthita Eka Pada Rajakapotasana).

Contraindications and Risks
- Contraindicated for students with shoulders, elbows, and wrist injuries.
- **Pregnancy**: Contraindicated for students who are pregnant.

Pendant Pose | Lolasana

low-lah-sah-nah

Starting Position

Begin in a kneeling stance.
Place your hands on the mat just outside your knees.
Press down into your hands and straighten your arms.

Proper Alignment

- **Feet**: Keep your feet together and lifted off the ground, engaging your leg muscles.
- **Legs**: Cross your legs, engage your inner thighs, and lift your knees towards your chest.
- **Hips**: Keep your hips lifted. Engage your abdominal muscles and lift the low pelvic floor, activating Uddiyana Bandha and Mula Bandha.
- **Torso**: Dome your upper back and contract your abdominal muscles, activating Uddiyana Bandha.
- **Arms**: Press your hands firmly into the mat.
- **Hands**: Ground down through your palms, pressing evenly through all four corners.
- **Gaze (Drishti):** Look slightly forward, keeping your neck long and neutral.

Modifications

- **Using Props**: Place a block under each hand for added support and lift.
- **Wrist Issues**: Avoid putting too much weight on your wrists. Modify by placing a folded mat or towel under them.
- **Shoulder Injuries**: Avoid putting too much weight on your shoulders. Focus on building strength gradually.

Contraindications and Risks

- Contraindicated for students with shoulders, elbows, and wrists injuries
- **Pregnancy**: Contraindicated for students who are pregnant

Eight Angle Pose I Astavakrasana

ahsh-tah-vah-krah-sah-nah

Starting Position

Begin in a seated position.

Bend your right knee and shift it back to slide your right shoulder under your knee. Press your knee down onto your shoulder for stability.

Press into your hands and lift your hips from the floor by contracting your abdominals for support.

Proper Alignment

- **Feet**: Hook your left foot over your right foot.
- **Legs**: Cross your legs, engage your inner thighs, and lift your knees towards your chest.
- **Hips**: Draw your hips straight back and reach the center of your sternum straight ahead.
- **Torso**: Twist your torso to the right, lengthening through your spine.
- **Arms**: Bend your elbows slightly, press your hands firmly into the mat, and spread your fingers wide.
- **Hands**: Ground down through your palms, pressing evenly through all four corners.
- **Gaze (Drishti)**: Look slightly forward, keeping your neck long and neutral.

Contraindications and Risks

- Contraindicated for students with shoulders, elbows, and wrist injuries.

225

Backbends

Backbends in yoga involve poses where the spine arches backward, opening the front body and stretching the muscles along the front of the torso.

All alignment instructions provided in this book are for the right side. In yoga practice, we often start with the right side, which is a tradition in many yoga classes. However, it is essential to always perform these poses on both sides to maintain balance in the body.

After completing the pose on the right side, please ensure you repeat the same pose on the left side, following the same alignment. Practicing on both sides will help you achieve a well-rounded and balanced practice, promoting symmetry and strength in your body.

Sphinx Pose I Salamba Bhujangasana

sah-lum-bah boo-jung-gah-sah-nah

Starting Position

Begin lying on your belly with your legs extended back and your feet hip-width apart.
Place your forearms on the mat, stack your elbows under your shoulders, elbows at a 90° angle.
Align your forearms parallel with each other onto the ground.

Proper Alignment

- **Feet**: Keep your feet hip-width apart and press the tops of your feet into the mat.
- **Legs**: Engage your quadriceps and lift your kneecaps off the mat.
- **Hips**: Press your pubic bone into the mat and lengthen your lower back by tilting your pelvis forward.
- **Torso**: Lift your chest, lengthening through your spine. Keep your lower ribs on the mat.
- **Arms**: Rest your forearms on the mat. Align your elbows under your shoulders and your forearms shoulder-width apart.
- **Hands**: Rest your palms flat on the mat and allow the fingers to spread and relax.
- **Gaze (Drishti):** Look ahead.

Contraindications and Risks

- **Pregnancy**: Contraindicated for students who are pregnant.

Cobra Pose | Bhujangasana

boo-jung-gah-sah-nuh

Starting Position

Begin in Chaturanga Dandasana or on your abdomen.
Press the tops of your feet onto the floor.
Plant your hands on the mat in alignment with your lower ribs.
Lift your chest and spread your collarbones.

Proper Alignment

- **Feet**: Keep your feet hip-width apart. Press the tops of your feet into the mat, spinning your pinky toes toward the mat.
- **Legs**: Engage your quadriceps and lift your kneecaps off the mat.
- **Hips**: Press your pubic bone into the mat and engage your lower abdomen.
- **Torso**: Lift your chest, lengthening through your spine.
- **Arms**: Press your hands firmly into the mat, keeping your elbows close to your body.
- **Hands**: Ground down through your palms, pressing evenly through all four corners.
- **Gaze**: Look slightly down or ahead to maintain a length in the back of your neck and a long cervical spine.

Modifications

- **Alternate Pose:** Students can do Urdhva Mukha Svanasana (Upward Facing Dog).

Contraindications and Risks

- **Pregnancy**: Contraindicated for students who are pregnant.

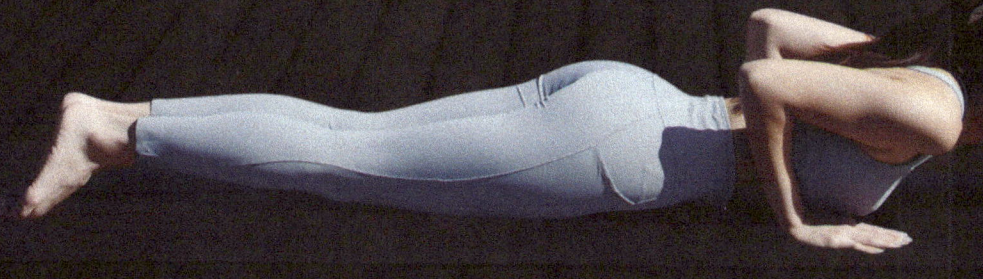

228

Upward Facing Dog | Urdhva Mukha Svanasana

oord-vah moo-khah shvah-nah-sah-nah

Starting Position
Begin in Bhujangasana (Cobra).
Press into your hands to straighten your arms.
Lift your knees off the mat and press through the tops of the feet.

Modifications
- **Alternative Pose:** Students have the option to do Bhujangasana (Cobra).

Contraindications and Risks
- **Lower Back Injuries**: Contraindicated for students with herniated discs.
- **Wrist Injuries**: Contraindicated for students with wrist injuries. Proceed with caution.

229

Cat Pose | Marjaryasana

mar-jar-ee-ah-sah-nah

Starting Position

Begin in Tabletop Position.

Round your spine towards the ceiling, tucking your chin to your chest.

Proper Alignment

- **Feet**: Keep your feet hip-width apart, pressing the tops of your feet into the mat.
- **Legs**: Stack your knees directly underneath your hips and keep them hip-width apart.
- **Hips**: Tuck your pelvis under, engaging your core and rounding your lower back.
- **Torso**: Round your spine towards the ceiling, engaging your upper back muscles. Engage your abdominal muscles and lift the low pelvic floor, activating Uddiyana Bandha and Mula Bandha. Tuck the chin toward the chest, activating Jalandhara Bandha (Throat Lock)
- **Arms**: Keep the arms straight with a direct line from shoulders to wrists.
- **Shoulders**: Spread your shoulder blades away from the spine.
- **Hands**: Separate the hands shoulder-distance apart and stack the wrists underneath the shoulders
- **Gaze (Drishti)**: Look towards your navel.

Contraindications and Risks

- **Neck Problems**: Keep your neck in a neutral position, avoiding excessive rounding.

Cow Pose | Bitilasana

bee-tee-lah-sah-nah

Starting Position
Begin in Tabletop Position.
Drop your belly down to arch your back towards the floor.
Lift your head and tailbone toward the sky.

Proper Alignment
- **Feet**: Keep your feet hip-width apart, pressing the tops of your feet into the mat.
- **Legs**: Stack your knees directly underneath your hips and keep them hip-width apart.
- **Hips**: Tilt your pelvis away from your face, creating an arch in your lower back.
- **Torso**: Arch your back towards the floor, engaging your upper back muscles. Feel the openness and stretch on the front side of your body.
- **Arms**: Keep the arms straight with a direct line from shoulders to wrists.
- **Shoulders**: Descend the shoulder blades toward the front of the chest and slide the shoulders down the back.
- **Hands**: Separate the hands shoulder-distance apart and stack the wrists underneath the shoulders
- **Gaze (Drishti):** Lift your head and look upward.

Contraindications and Risks
- **Neck Problems**: Keep your neck in a neutral position, avoiding excessive rounding.

Reclining Hero's Pose | Supta Virasana

soop-tah veer-ah-sah-nah

Starting Position
Begin in Virasana (Hero's Pose).
Lean back on your forearms.
If your knees do not lift off the ground, continue to lean onto your back as far as possible.

Proper Alignment
- **Feet**: Separate your feet wider than your hips, and rest the tops of the feet outside of your hips and on the earth.
- **Legs**: Bring the knees together to touch and engage your quadriceps and inner thighs.
- **Hips**: Sit your hips between your ankles or on a yoga block.
- **Torso**: Sit upright, stacking the shoulders above the hips—option to lean back, lowering your upper body to the mat. If the knees begin to lift off the mat, that is a sign that you went too far.
- **Arms**: Gently rest your hands on your thighs or knees. If you recline onto your back, you can extend your arms by your side or reach the arms over the head and hold opposite elbows, creating a frame around the head.

Modifications
- **Alternative Pose:** If lying down is too much, stay in Virasana (Hero's Pose).
- **Knee Problems**: Use caution and avoid placing too much weight on your knees. If your knees begin to lift off the yoga mat, that is a sign that you are straining them.

Contraindications and Risks
- **Lower Back Injuries**: Contraindicated for students with herniated discs.
- **Ankle Issues:** Contraindicated for students with ankle injuries. Proceed with caution.

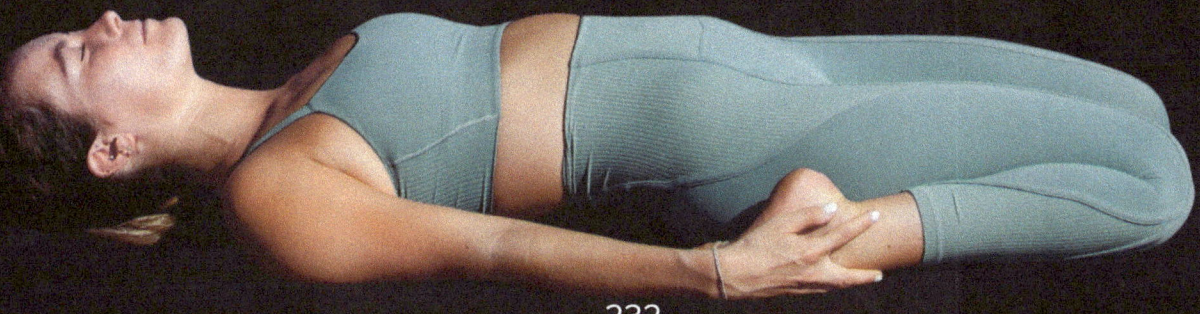

Locust Pose | Salabhasana

shah-lah-bah-sah-nah

Starting Position

Begin lying on your abdomen with your legs extended back and your arms along your sides.

Lift your head, chest, and legs off the mat.

Reach your arms back.

Proper Alignment

- **Feet**: Keep your feet together and lift them off the mat.
- **Legs**: Engage your quadriceps and inner thighs, lifting your legs.
- **Hips**: Balance on your frontal hip bones, engaging your core and lower back muscles.
- **Torso**: Peel your chest off the mat, lengthening through your spine.
- **Arms**: Reach your arms back, palms facing upwards or inwards.
- **Shoulders**: Roll the shoulders back, spread wide through the collarbones, and lift the chest.
- **Hands**: Keep your fingers extended and active, reaching towards your feet.
- **Gaze (Drishti)**: Look slightly down, keeping the back of the neck long and relaxed.

Contraindications and Risks

- **Pregnancy**: Contraindicated for students who are pregnant.

Bow Pose | Dhanurasana
dah-noo-rah-sah-nah

Starting Position
Begin lying on your belly with your legs extended back and your arms along your sides.
Bend your knees so that the soles of your feet face the sky.
Reach back to grasp your ankles.

Proper Alignment
- **Feet**: Keep your feet flexed to protect your knees.
- **Legs**: Separate your legs hip-distance apart and engage your quadriceps and inner thighs. Imagine a yoga block between your inner thighs as you hug the block. Lift your quads up and your shins back.
- **Hips**: Engage your glute muscles.
- **Torso**: Lift your chest and spread your collarbone from shoulder to shoulder. Lengthen through your spine.
- **Arms**: Reach your arms back and grasp your ankles or feet. Feel the extension and energy in your arms.

- **Arms**: Reach your arms back and grasp your ankles or feet. Feel the extension and energy in your arms.
- **Hands**: Like a bow and an arrow, kick the feet into the hands, creating a solid connection. Keep your grip firm but gentle, pressing your feet into your hands.
- **Gaze (Drishti):** Look slightly forward, keeping your neck long and relaxed.

Modifications
- **Using Props**: Use a yoga block between your inner thighs or maintain Salabhasana (Locust Pose).

Contraindications and Risks
- **Lower Back Injuries**: Contraindicated for students with herniated discs.
- **Pregnancy**: Contraindicated for students who are pregnant.
- **Medical Complications:** Contraindicated for students who have a history of high blood pressure, stroke, or heart disease.

Half Frog Pose | Ardha Bhekasana
ar-dha bay-kuh-sah-nah

Starting Position
Begin in Salamba Bhujangasana (Sphinx Pose).
Bend your right knee.
Externally rotate your right palm and reach back to grasp the right foot from the inside edge.
Spiral your right elbow up to the sky and press the heel of the palm on top of the foot.

Proper Alignment
- **Feet:** Keep your left leg extended and press the top of your left foot into the mat. Keep the top of the right foot pressing against your right palm.
- **Legs:** Engage your quadriceps and inner thighs to lift your right knee off the mat. Draw your right foot outside of your right hip as you press the foot gently down into the earth.
- **Hips:** Press your pubic bone into the mat, engaging your core and stabilizing your hips.
- **Torso:** Keep your torso facing the front of your yoga mat. Lift your chest off the mat, lengthening through your spine. Keep your lower ribs on the mat.
- **Arms:** Keep your left elbow above your shoulder as you push the floor away from you with your left forearm. Avoid collapsing down into the left shoulder.
- **Hands:** Keep a firm but gentle grip on your right foot. Press your left palm into the mat for support.
- **Gaze (Drishti):** Look ahead to keep from rotating your chest to one side. Keep your neck long and relaxed.

Modifications
- **Alternative Pose:** Students can hold Salamba Bhujangasana (Sphinx Pose).
- **Knee Problems**: Use caution and avoid placing too much strain on your knee.
- **Shoulder Issues**: Avoid overextending your shoulder or collapsing to one shoulder.

Contraindications and Risks
- **Lower Back Injuries:** Contraindicated for students with herniated discs.
- **Specific Medical Needs:** This pose is contraindicated for students with high or low blood pressure.

236

Upward Facing Plank | Purvottanasana
poor-vo-tun-ah-sah-nah

Starting Position
Begin in Dandasana (Staff Pose).
Place your hands directly underneath the shoulders.
Extend your legs straight as you rest the soles of your feet on the earth.
Lift your hips towards the sky.

Proper Alignment
- **Feet**: Point your toes and gently press the soles of your feet into the mat.
- **Legs**: Engage your quadriceps and inner thighs, lifting your hips up.
- **Hips**: Lift your hips off the mat, engaging your glute muscles.
- **Torso**: Lift your chest towards the sky, lengthening through your spine. Engage your abdominal muscles.
- **Arms**: Press your hands firmly into the mat, keeping your elbows straight and your shoulders open. Keep a direct line from your shoulders to your wrists.
- **Hands**: Ground down through your palms. Point the fingertips toward your toes.
- **Gaze (Drishti):** Look up towards the sky, keeping your neck long and relaxed.

Modifications
- **Alternative Pose:** Bend your knees and keep your feet flat on the floor, hip-distance apart, as the hips lift.
- **Wrists:** Rotate your fingertips to face the outer sides of the mat.

Contraindications and Risks
- Contraindicated for students with shoulders, elbows and wrist injuries.

237

Camel Pose | Ustrasana
oos-trah-sah-nah

Starting Position
Begin standing on your knees, stacking your shoulders over your hips and your hips over your knees.
Place your hands on your hips or lower back, with your fingertips pointing down.
Press your hips forward and lift your chest towards the sky, feeling the expansive opening in your heart center and the grounding stability through your legs.

Proper Alignment
- **Feet**: Gently rest the tops of your feet into the mat or tuck your toes under.
- **Legs**: Keep your thighs hip-distance apart, as if there were a yoga block between your inner thighs and you are hugging it inward. Engage your quadriceps and send your hips forward.
- **Hips**: Press your hips forward, engaging your glutes and abdominal muscles.
- **Torso**: Lift your chest towards the sky, lengthening through your spine.
- **Arms**: Option to reach back with your hands to grasp your heels or keep your hands on your lower back for support.
- **Hands**: Keep a firm but gentle grip on your heels, or rest your hands on your lower back.
- **Gaze (Drishti):** Tuck your chin slightly towards your chest to avoid straining the cervical spine and activating your limbic system, which triggers your flight or fight response.

Modifications

- **Using Props**: Place a blanket under your knees for added support.
- **Alternative Pose:** Keep your hands on your lower back for added support.

Contraindications and Risks

- **Lower Back Injuries**: Contraindicated for students with herniated discs.
- **Specific Medical Needs**: Contraindicated for students with high blood pressure, heart disease, or a history of stroke.

Fish Pose I Matsyasana
maht-see-ah-sah-nah

Starting Position
Begin lying on your back with your legs extended and your arms by your sides.
Come on to your elbows as you slide your hands under the sacrum with your palms facing down, making a diamond shape with your two hands.
Lift your chest, open your throat, and place the crown of your head on the mat.

Proper Alignment
- **Feet**: Keep your legs extended and point through your toes.
- **Legs**: Engage your quadriceps and inner thigh muscles.
- **Hips**: Lift your hips slightly off the mat to slide your hands underneath.
- **Torso**: Lift your chest towards the sky, lengthening through your spine.
- **Arms**: Keep a bend in your elbows.
- **Hands**: Plant the palms down under the sacrum. Bring both hands' thumbs and index fingers together, creating a diamond shape.
- **Gaze (Drishti)**: Look back or close your eyes.

Contraindications and Risks
- **Neck Pain**: Contraindicated for students with neck pain.
- **Lower Back Injuries:** Contraindicated for students with herniated discs.
- Contraindicated for students with shoulders, elbows, and wrist injuries.
- **Specific Medical Needs:** Contraindicated for students with high blood pressure or a history of heart disease. Proceed cautiously.

Modifications

- **Hamstring Tightness**: Use a strap around your right foot if you cannot reach your big toe.
- **Slight Bend:** Maintain a slight bend in the knee to avoid hyperextension.

Contraindications and Risks

- **Pregnancy**: Contraindicated for pregnant students who can no longer lift their legs.

Bridge Pose | Setu Bandha Sarvangasana

say-tuh bun-duh sar-vun-gah-sah-nah

Starting Position

Begin lying on your back with your knees bent and your feet flat on the mat, hip-width apart. Press into your heels and lift your hips towards the sky.

Proper Alignment

- **Feet**: Keep your feet hip-width apart and press them firmly into the mat.
- **Legs**: Stack your knees above your ankles. Engage your quadriceps and inner thigh muscles, as if there was a yoga block between your inner thighs, activating the adductor muscles. Lift your hips upwards.
- **Hips**: Lift your hips off the mat, engaging your glutes and abdominal muscles. Tuck your tailbone under to lengthen your sacrum. Scoop your pelvis toward the face, activating Mula Bandha.
- **Torso**: Hug your lower ribs inward toward your spine, activating Uddiyana Bandha. Lengthen through your spine, lifting your chest towards your chin.
- **Arms**: Extend your arms along the mat, palms facing down, or clasp your hands under your back.
- **Hands**: Ground down through your palms, pressing evenly through all four corners. Students can interlace their fingers under their lower back to help draw their shoulder blades under their chest and lift through the back of their heart.
- **Gaze (Drishti)**: Look up towards the sky, keeping your neck long and relaxed.

Modifications

- **Alternative Pose:** Students unable to perform the pose can place a yoga block at the lowest height horizontally underneath the sacrum, arriving at a Supported Bridge Pose (Salamba Setu Bandha Sarvangasana).

Contraindications and Risks

- **Neck Injuries**: Contraindicated for students with neck injuries.

Upward Facing Wheel Pose | Urdhva Dhanurasana

oord-vah dah-noo-rah-sah-nah

Starting Position

Begin in Setu Bandha Sarvangasana (Bridge Pose).
Place your hands on the mat beside your ears, fingers pointing towards your shoulders.
When ready, lift your hips off the mat.

Proper Alignment

- **Feet**: Keep your feet hip-width apart and your toes pointing straight forward.
- **Legs**: Engage your quadriceps and inner thighs as if there were a yoga block between your thighs, activating the adductor muscles.
- **Hips**: Lift your hips off the mat, engaging your glute muscles.
- **Torso**: Open the front chain of the body. Lengthen through your spine, lifting your chest towards the sky. Draw the front ribs toward the front hip points and breathe into your chest.
- **Arms**: Hug the elbows in toward each other. Press your hands firmly into the mat, straightening your arms.
- **Hands**: Ground down through your palms, pressing evenly through all four corners.
- **Gaze (Drishti):** Look slightly forward or up, allowing your head to hang.

Modifications

- **Using Props**: Use a strap above the elbows for extra security to prevent them from flaring outward. Place a yoga block between the inner thighs.
- **Alternative Pose:** You have the option to stay in Setu Bandha Sarvangasana (Bridge Pose) instead.

Contraindications and Risks

Lower Back Injuries: Contraindicated for students with herniated discs. Contraindicated for students with shoulders, elbows, and wrist injuries.
Specific Medical Needs: Contraindicated for students with high blood pressure, glaucoma, or a history of stroke or heart disease.

Upward Facing Two-Foot Staff Pose | Dwi Pada Viparita Dandasana

dwee pah-duh vee-puh-ree-tuh dun-dah-sah-nah

Starting Position

Begin in Urdhva Dhanurasana (Upward Facing Bow Pose).

Lower your forearms to the mat, keeping your elbows shoulder-width apart.

Lift your head from the floor.

Modifications

- **Using Props**: Use a strap above the elbows for extra security to prevent them from flaring outward.
- **Alternative Pose:** You have the option of staying in Setu Bandha Sarvangasana (Bridge Pose).

Contraindications and Risks

- **Lower Back Injuries:** Contraindicated for students with herniated discs.
- Contraindicated for students with shoulders, elbows, and wrist injuries.
- **Specific Medical Needs:** Contraindicated for students with high blood pressure, glaucoma, or a history of stroke or heart disease.

245

Seated Postures and Forward Bends

Seated postures in yoga involve sitting on the ground. Forward bends involve folding from the hips, reaching toward the feet or the floor. Both seated postures and forward bends are commonly practiced toward the end of a yoga session to prepare the body for relaxation and meditation.

All alignment instructions provided in this book are for the right side. In yoga practice, we often start with the right side, which is a tradition in many yoga classes. However, it is essential always to perform these poses on both sides to maintain balance in the body.

After completing the pose on the right side, please ensure you repeat the same pose on the left side, following the exact alignment. Practicing on both sides will help you achieve a well-rounded and balanced practice, promoting symmetry and strength in your body.

Staff Pose | Dandasana

dahn-dah-sah-nah

Starting Position

Begin seated, stacking your head about your shoulders and shoulders above your hips. Extend both legs straight forward, actively flex your feet, and engage your quadriceps.

Proper Alignment

- **Feet**: Bring the inner edges of your feet to connect. Spiral the inner edges forward and away from you and the outer edges backward toward your face. Flex your feet.
- **Legs**: Draw your kneecaps up while engaging your quadriceps and inner thighs, pressing the backs of your legs into the mat.
- **Hips**: Stack the hips underneath the shoulders.
- **Torso**: Lengthen through your spine as you draw your belly in and lift through the crown of your head.
- **Arms**: Place your hands on the mat beside your hips, pressing down to lift your chest.
- **Shoulders**: Stack your shoulders directly over your hips and slide your shoulder blades down your back.
- **Hands**: Ground down through your palms, pressing evenly through all four corners.
- **Gaze (Drishti):** Look straight ahead, keeping your neck long and relaxed.

Modifications

- **Using Props:** If the lower back rounds. Place a folded blanket under the sit bones to help lift out the lower back and tilt the pelvis slightly forward.
- **Slight Bend:** Add a slight bend to your knees to reduce strain on your lower back and hamstrings.

Head to Knee Pose | Janu Sirsasana

jah-noo sheer-shah-sah-nah

Starting Position
- Begin in Dandasana (Staff Pose).
- Bend your right knee.
- Place the sole of your right foot against your left inner thigh.

Proper Alignment
- **Feet**: Flex your extended left foot, pressing through your heel and engaging your leg muscles. Keep the foot of your bent right leg pressing into your extended leg's inner thigh.
- **Legs**: Engage your quadriceps and inner thighs, pressing the backs of your legs into the mat.
- **Hips**: Keep your hips in a neutral rotation facing forward.
- **Torso**: Lengthen through your spine, reaching forward over your extended left leg. Engage your abdominal muscles and lift the low pelvic floor, activating Uddiyana Bandha and Mula Bandha to support your lower back.
- **Arms**: Extend your arms forward, reaching for your foot or shins. Allow your elbows to bend slightly, freeing your neck and shoulders.
- **Hands**: Hold your foot, ankle, or shin, pressing back gently to deepen the stretch.
- **Gaze (Drishti)**: Look down toward your knee, keeping the back of the] neck long and relaxed.

Modifications
- **Using Props**: If the lower back rounds, place a folded blanket under the sit bones to help lift out the lower back and tilt the pelvis slightly forward. Use a strap around the sole of the right foot.
- **Slight Bend**: Add a slight bend to your knee to reduce strain on your lower back and hamstrings.

Contraindications and Risks
- **Hamstring Injuries**: Use caution and avoid overstretching your hamstrings, modifying with a folded blanket under your hips.
- **Lower Back Pain**: Keep the spine straight and chest elevated to avoid rounding if you have a herniated disc.

Seated Forward Fold | Paschimottanasana

pash-chee-moh-tuh-nah-sah-nah

Starting Position

Begin in Dandasana (Staff Pose).
Sweep your arms overhead, drawing your shoulders down.
Lengthen through your spine and fold forward over your legs.

Proper Alignment

- **Feet**: Bring the inner edges of your feet to connect. Spiral the inner edges forward and away from you and the outer edges backward toward your face. Flex your feet.
- **Legs**: Draw your kneecaps up while engaging your quadriceps and inner thighs, pressing the backs of your legs into the mat.
- **Hips**: Hinge at your hips, keeping your spine long and engaging your core.
- **Torso**: Lengthen through your spine, keeping your cervical spine in line with the rest of the spine.
- **Arms**: Extend your arms forward, reaching for your feet or shins.
- **Hands**: Hold your feet, ankles, or shins, pressing gently to deepen the stretch.
- **Gaze (Drishti):** Look towards your feet, keeping your neck long and relaxed.

Modifications

- **Using Props:** Use a strap around your feet to make the pose more accessible, or consider sitting on a folded blanket to aid lower back pain or tight hamstrings.

Contraindications and Risks

- **Hamstring Tightness**: Avoid overstretching your hamstrings, modifying with a strap or blanket.
- **Back Pain**: Contraindicated for students with back pain caused by herniated or bulging discs. Students with lower back pain or tightness should keep the spine long and chest elevated.

251

Bound Angle Pose | Baddha Konasana
bah-dah cone-ah-sah-nah

Starting Position
Begin in Dandasana (Staff Pose).
Bend your knees and bring the soles of your feet together, allowing your knees to drop out to the sides
Lengthen through your spine and fold between your legs.

Proper Alignment
- **Feet**: Bring the soles of your feet together and hook your two peace fingers around the big toes.
- **Legs**: Allow your knees to open out to the sides, engaging your inner thighs, sensing the opening and support.
- **Torso**: Hing from the hips and lengthen through your spine, lifting through the crown of your head, feeling the openness and extension.
- **Arms**: Press your elbows against the inner thighs to open the legs. Avoid putting the elbows on the knees.
- **Hands**: Ground down through your sitting bones and hold your feet or ankles, feeling the stability and grounding.
- **Gaze (Drishti):** Look straight ahead, keeping your neck long and relaxed.

Modifications
- **Using Props**: Place a blanket or blocks under your knees for added support to elevate your hips and reduce strain on your lower back.

Contraindications and Risks
- **Knee Injuries**: This pose is contraindicated for students with knee injuries.
- **Lower Back Pain**: Engage your core to support your lower back, avoiding rounding the spine.

Spread Leg Forward Fold | Upavistha Konasana
oo-pah-veesh-tah cone-ah-sah-nah

Starting Position
Begin in Dandasana (Staff Pose).
Spread your legs apart, keeping them active as your thighs firm and feet flex.
Lengthen through your spine and fold between your legs, feeling the expansive opening in your hips and the grounding connection through your sitting bones.

Proper Alignment
- **Feet**: Flex your feet, pressing through your heels and engaging your leg muscles.
- **Legs**: Engage your quadriceps and inner thighs, pressing the backs of your legs into the mat.
- **Hips**: Hinge at your hips, keeping your spine long and engaging your core.
- **Torso**: Align your torso directly over your sacrum, rooting your sit bones down. Extend your torso forward, keeping your spine lengthened and straight by engaging Uddiyana Bandha and Mula Bandha. Engage your core to support your lower back, avoiding rounding and maintaining stability.
- **Arms**: Extend your arms forward, reaching for your feet or the mat.
- Shoulders: Draw your shoulder blades away from your ears and extend your sternum forward as your chest opens.
- Hands: Hook your big toes with your two peace fingers, hold your ankles or shins, or press your hands into the mat.
- Gaze (Drishti): Look towards the mat, keeping your neck long and relaxed.

253

Modifications

- **Using Props:** Sit on a folded blanket to elevate your hips and make the pose more accessible.
- **Slight Bend:** Add a slight bend to your knees to reduce strain on your lower back and hamstrings.
- **Back Pain**: Students with back pain, bulging, or herniated discs should keep their spines upright.

Contraindications and Risks

- **Groin injuries:** Contraindicated for students with groin injuries. Proceed with caution.

Boat Pose | Navasana
nah-vah-sah-nah

Starting Position
Begin in Dandasana (Staff Pose).
Root your sit bones to the floor.
Extend your feet off the mat to create a "V" shape with your torso and legs. Extend your arms forward to be parallel to the ground.

Proper Alignment
- **Feet**: Lift your feet off the mat, keeping them together and parallel to the ground. Press the balls of your feet forward while spreading your toes.
- **Legs**: Engage your quadriceps and inner thighs, straightening your legs if possible.
- **Hips**: Balance your weight on your hips.
- **Torso**: Engage your abdominal muscles and lift the low pelvic floor, activating Uddiyana Bandha and Mula Bandha. Lengthen through your spine, keeping the chest open, and lift.
- **Arms**: Extend your arms forward, parallel to the ground.
- **Shoulders**: Draw your shoulder blades down your back and spread your collarbones while lifting your heart to the sky.
- **Hands**: Palms face each other.
- **Gaze (Drishti):** Look straight ahead, keeping your neck long and relaxed.

Modifications
- **Bend Knees**: Keep your knees bent and hold the backs of your thighs for added support.
- **Hands:** Students can place their hands on the floor or behind their thighs for support.

Contraindications and Risks
- **Tailbone Injuries:** Contraindicated for students who have tailbone injuries.
- **Specific Medical Needs:** This pose is contraindicated for students with low blood pressure and heart problems.
- **Pregnancy:** Students who are pregnant should proceed with caution.

Child's Pose | Balasana
bah-lah-sah-nah

Proper Alignment
- **Feet**: Keep your big toes together and your knees wide apart, pressing the tops of your feet into the mat.
- **Legs**: Allow your hips to sink back towards your heels. Rest the inner thighs against your ribcage.
- **Hips**: Rest your hips on your heels or on a yoga block.
- **Torso**: Lengthen through your spine, reaching forward with your arms and lowering your chest to the mat.
- **Arms**: Extend your arms forward or rest your arms by your sides.
- **Hands**: Ground down through your palms, with the palms facing down.
- **Gaze (Drishti):** Rest your forehead on the mat, keeping your neck long and relaxed.

Modifications
- **Using Props**: Place a blanket or bolster under your knees for added support. Use a block underneath your forehead for support if your head does not reach the mat. Place a block horizontally between your ankles, and sit on it if your hips can't reach your heels.
- **Gentle Modification:** Keep the rounding in the spine and a soft bend in the elbows.

Contraindications and Risks
- **Knee Problems**: Use caution and avoid placing too much strain on your knees, modifying with a blanket or bolster.

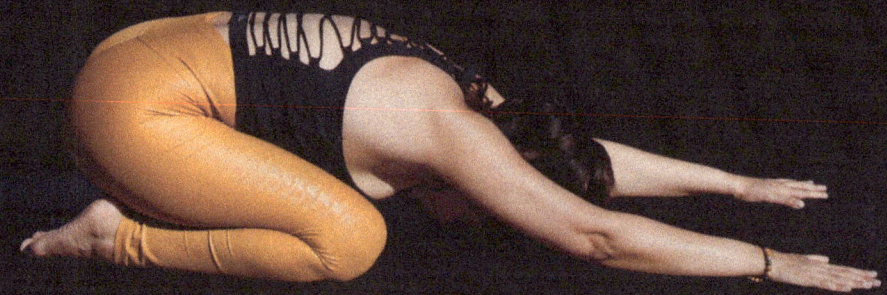

257

Hero's Pose | Virasana
veer-ah-sah-nah

Starting Position
Begin in a kneeling position with your knees together and your feet wider than your hips. Move the flesh of your calf muscles back to make space for your thighs before lowering your sit bones down.

Sit back between your heels, keeping your spine tall.

Proper Alignment
- **Feet**: Keep your feet wider than the hips, pressing the tops of your feet into the mat as the pinkie toes spin down.
- **Legs**: Engage your quadriceps and inner thighs, keeping your knees together.
- **Hips**: Sit back between your heels.
- **Torso**: Lengthen through your spine, lifting through the crown of your head. Engage your core and lengthen your spine.
- **Shoulders**: Stack your shoulders over your hips.
- **Hands**: Place your hands on your thighs, palms facing down, or in a prayer position at your heart.
- **Gaze (Drishti):** Look straight ahead, keeping your neck long and relaxed.

Modifications
- **Using Props:** Place a block, blanket, or bolster under your sit bones for added support.
- **Alternative Pose:** If there is pain in your knees even with the use of supportive props, students are welcome to do Sukhasana (Cross Leg Seated Pose) as a modification.

Contraindications and Risks
- Contraindicated for students with knee and ankle injury.

Crossed Leg Seated Pose | Sukhasana

soo-kah-sah-nah

Starting Position
Begin in a seated position.
Align your head above your shoulders, and your shoulders above your hips.
Cross your shins against each other, bringing each foot beneath the opposite knee.

Proper Alignment
- **Feet**: Actively flex your feet to protect your knees.
- **Legs**: Allow your knees to drop out to the sides, engaging your inner thighs.
- **Hips**: Stack the hips underneath the shoulders and distribute your weight evenly on both hips.
- **Torso**: Lengthen through your spine, lifting through the crown of your head. Engage your abdominal muscles and lift the low pelvic floor, activating Uddiyana Bandha and Mula Bandha.
- **Arms**: Soften your elbows to minimize tension in your arms and shoulders.
- **Shoulders**: Stack your shoulders over your hips. Draw your shoulders down your back.
- **Hands**: Rest your hands on your knees or in a prayer position in Anjali Mudra.
- **Gaze (Drishti)**: Look straight ahead, keeping your neck long and relaxed

Modifications
- **Using Props:** Place a blanket or bolster under your sit bones to elevate your hips higher than your knees for added support. Alternatively, yoga blocks may be placed under the knees for additional support.

Lotus | Padmasana

pahd-mah-sah-nah

Starting Position

Begin in Dandasana (Staff Pose).

Place your right foot on your left thigh as close to the hip crease as possible, with the sole facing up.

Bring your left foot across and place it on your right thigh, as close to the hip crease as possible, with the sole facing up.

Proper Alignment

- **Feet**: Keep the soles of your feet facing up toward the sky and stack them above the femur.
- **Legs**: Cross the shins on top of each other and allow the knees to open to the sides.
- **Hips**: Sit in a neutral position with your pelvis, ensuring that your sit bones are grounded evenly on the mat.
- **Torso**: Lengthen through your spine, lifting through the crown of your head while grounding through your sit bones, keeping a vertical line from crown to tail. Engage your abdominal muscles and lift the low pelvic floor, activating Uddiyana Bandha and Mula Bandha.
- **Hands**: Rest your hands on your knees. You can form a mudra (e.g., Gyan Mudra) by touching the tips of your thumbs and index fingers together.

260

- **Shoulders**: Stack the shoulders above the hips. Relax your shoulders away from your ears, keeping your chest open and broad.
- **Gaze (Drishti)**: Maintain a soft gaze straight ahead or close your eyes for a more meditative experience.

Modifications

- **Using Props**: Place a blanket or bolster under your hips for added support.
- **Alternative Pose**: Practice Half Lotus by placing one foot on the opposite thigh and the other foot under the opposite knee.

Contraindications and Risks

- **Knee Injuries**: Contraindicated for students with knee injuries.

Hip Opener and Seated Twists

Hip openers in yoga are poses that target the muscles around the hips, such as the hip flexors, glutes, and outer hips. These poses help to increase flexibility and mobility in the hip joints, alleviate tightness, and improve posture.

Seated twists in yoga are poses where practitioners twist their torso while seated on the ground. These poses provide a gentle massage to the abdominal organs, improve spinal mobility, and release tension in the back and shoulders. Seated twists also help to detoxify the body by stimulating digestion and promoting the elimination of waste.

All alignment instructions provided in this book are for the right side. In yoga practice, we often start with the right side, which is a tradition in many yoga classes. However, it is essential to always perform these poses on both sides to maintain balance in the body.

After completing the pose on the right side, please ensure you repeat the same pose on the left side, following the same alignment. Practicing on both sides will help you achieve a well-rounded and balanced practice, promoting symmetry and strength in your body.

Pigeon I Eka Pada Rajakapotasana

ek-uh pah-duh rah-juh-kahp-oh-tahs-uh-nuh

Starting Position

Begin in Adho Mukha Svanasana (Downward Facing Dog) and lift your right leg up.
Bring your right knee forward toward the front right edge of the mat.
Extend your left leg back.

Proper Alignment

- **Feet:** Flex your right foot to activate your shin and protect your knee.
- **Legs:** Align your shin to the front of your yoga mat as much as possible. Engage the inner thighs by hugging the adductor muscles in toward each other. Extend your left leg straight back, keeping the top of the foot flat on the floor, to stretch the psoas muscle and quadriceps of the left leg.
- **Hips:** Externally rotate through the right hip. Distribute your weight evenly on both hips to keep them level.
- **Torso:** Lift your chest and lengthen through your spine, reaching up and back. Engage your abdominal muscles and lift the low pelvic floor, activating Uddiyana Bandha and Mula Bandha.
- **Hands:** Place your hands on the mat by your sides.
- **Gaze (Drishti):** Look slightly forward or down, keeping your neck long and relaxed.

Modifications

- Using Props: Place a block, folded blanket, or bolster under the right hip to avoid titling too much to one hip.
- Alternative Pose: Students with knee or ankle discomfort may choose to perform Reclining Pigeon (Thread the Needle).

Contraindications and Risks

- Contraindicated for students with knee, hip, and ankle injuries.

Pigeon II | Eka Pada Rajakapotasana II

ek-uh pah-duh rah-juh-kahp-oh-tah-sah-nah

Starting Position

Begin in Eka Pada Rajakapotasana (Pigeon I).

Bend your left knee.

Reach for your left foot. Holding the outer edge of the foot, spin the tip of your elbow to the sky.

Proper Alignment

- **Feet**: Keep your right foot flexed, and your left foot pointed, pressing the tops of your feet into the mat.
- **Legs**: Engage your quadriceps and inner thighs. Your right knee should be outside your right wrist, and your left leg should be extended straight back.
- **Hips**: Square your hips towards the front of the mat, engaging your core to support your lower back.
- **Torso**: Lift your chest and lengthen through your spine, reaching up and back.
- **Arms**: Extend your right arm overhead or place your hand on your front thigh for support.
- **Hands**: Reach up with your left hand or press gently into your front thigh with your right hand.
- **Gaze (Drishti)**: Look slightly forward or up, maintaining a long neck and relaxed jaw.

Modifications

- Students can stay in Pigeon I (Eka Pada Rajakapotasana I)

Contraindications and Risks

- **Lower Back Injuries:** Contraindicated for students with herniated discs.
- Contraindicated for students with shoulders, elbows, and wrist injuries.

Pigeon | Kapotasana

Starting Position
Begin in Eka Pada Rajakapotasana I (Pigeon Pose).
Lower your torso over your front leg.
Rest your forehead on the mat or a yoga block.
Extend your arms forward, or keep the elbows bent.

Cow Face Pose | Gomukhasana

go-moo-kah-sah-nah

Starting Position

Begin on all fours, cross your right knee in front of your left knee and sit back.
Hug the inner thighs toward each other while spreading your feet wider than your hips.

Proper Alignment

- **Feet:** Flex both feet.
- **Legs:** Stack your right knee above your left knee. Hug the inner thighs inward toward each other, internally rotating through the legs.
- **Hips:** Distribute your weight evenly on both hips.
- **Torso:** Lengthen through your spine, lifting through the crown of your head.
- **Arms:** Extend your right arm up as you bend your elbow, reaching the hand down your back. Reach your left arm behind your back and clasp your hands.
- **Hands:** Clasp your hands behind your back, keeping your grip firm but gentle.
- **Gaze (Drishti):** Look straight ahead, keeping your neck long and relaxed.

Modifications

- **Using Props**: If you cannot clasp your hands together, use a strap to connect them. Place a block or folded blanket under your hips for added support.

Contraindications and Risks

- Contraindicated for students with shoulder, knee, and foot injuries.

Garland Pose | Malasana

mah-lah-sah-nah

Starting Position

Begin in Uttanasana (Forward Fold).
Spread your feet wider than your hips, and turn your toes out.
Bend your knees and lower your hips into a squat, bringing your hands to your heart in prayer, Anjali Mudra.

Proper Alignment

- **Feet**: Externally rotate your feet, spinning the toes out and the heels in. Keep them wider than your hips. If your heels lift off the floor, spread your feet wider. If your heels still do not touch the floor, roll a blanket or part of your yoga mat under your heels for support.
- **Legs**: Bend your knees deeply, bringing your hips close to your heels.
- **Hips**: Lower your hips towards your heels, engaging your core and lengthening your spine. Lift the low pelvic floor, activating Mula Bandha.
- **Torso**: Lengthen through your spine, lifting through the crown of your head. Engage your abdominal muscles by activating Uddiyana Bandha.
- **Arms**: Press your elbows into your inner thighs to open the legs. Never push the knees.
- **Shoulders**: Soften your shoulders down your back to keep the neck long.
- **Hands**: Bring your palms together for a prayer gesture, Anjali Mudra.
- **Gaze (Drishti)**: Look straight ahead, keeping your neck long and relaxed.

Modifications

- **Using Props**: Place a yoga block or rolled-up blanket under your sit bones for added support.
- **Knee Pain**: Avoid placing too much strain on your knees, modifying with support under your hips.
- **Hip Problems**: Use caution and avoid overstretching your hips, modifying with support as needed.

Contraindications and Risks

- Contraindicated for students with knee, ankle, and foot injuries.

Frog | Mandukasana

mahn-doo-kah-sah-nah

Starting Position

Begin on all fours, facing the long side of your yoga mat.
Open your knees as wide as they will part, bringing your ankles in line with your knees.
Flex your feet and spread them wider than your knees.

Proper Alignment

- **Feet**: Keep your feet flexed and vertically aligned with your knees. Rest the inner edges of the feet onto the mat.
- **Legs**: Keep a 90° angle shape in your knees. Engage your inner thighs.
- **Hips**: Keep your hips horizontally aligned with your knees. Tilt your tailbone upward.
- **Torso**: Lengthen through your spine, lowering your chest towards the mat.
- **Arms**: Lower your forearms down to the mat, aligning your shoulders above your elbows.
- **Hands**: Rest your palms on the earth or interlace the fingers.
- **Gaze (Drishti):** Look down towards the mat, keeping the back of your neck long and relaxed.

Modifications

- **Using Props**: For added support, place a blanket under your knees, a yoga block under your forehead, or a bolster under your torso.

Contraindications and Risks

- **Specific Medical Needs:** Contraindicated for students with herniated discs or knee injuries.

269

Half Splits | Ardha Hanumanasana
ard-ha hah-noo-mahn-ah-sah-nah

Starting Position
Begin in Anjaneyasana (Low Lunge) with your right foot forward.
Straighten your right leg ahead of you.
Hinge from the hips and fold over your right leg.

Proper Alignment
- **Feet:** Keep your right foot flexed, pressing the heel into the mat.
- **Legs:** Engage your quadriceps and inner thighs, straightening your right leg while keeping your left knee bent and grounded.
- **Hips:** Hinge at the hips to fold forward over your right leg. Square your hips towards the front of the mat, engaging your core to support your lower back.
- **Torso:** Align your torso over your right leg as you open your chest and lengthen through your spine.
- **Hands:** Place your hands on the mat above your shoulders on either side of your right leg, or extend them forward to deepen the stretch.
- **Gaze (Drishti):** Look slightly down towards your right leg, keeping the back of the neck long and relaxed.

Modifications
- **Using Props**: Place blocks under your hands for added support, or place a blanket underneath your knee.

Contraindications and Risks
- **Specific Medical Needs**: Contraindicated for students with bulged or herniated discs.

Splits | Hanumanasana

hah-noo-mahn-ah-sah-nah

Starting Position

Begin in Half Splits (Ardha Hanumanasana).

Lift your chest to an upright position.

Extend your back left leg toward straight.

Keep your hips level with each other and in a neutral rotation.

Modifications

- **Alternative Pose**: Stay in Half Splits (Ardha Hanumanasana).

Contraindications and Risks

- **Specific Medical Needs**: Contraindicated for students with sciatica, bulged or herniated discs.

271

Double Seated Pigeon | Agnistambhasana

ahg-nee-stahm-bah-sah-nah

Starting Position

Begin in Dandasana (Staff Pose).

Bend your knees and stack your right shin on top of your left shin, bringing your right ankle to rest on your left knee and your left ankle to rest on your right knee.

Proper Alignment

- **Feet**: Flex both feet to protect your knees. Align your feet with your knees.
- **Legs**: Stack your shins parallel with each other, creating space between your inner thighs.
- **Hips**: Externally rotate through the outer hips.
- **Torso**: Stack the head above the shoulders and shoulders above the hips, keeping the spine vertically aligned.
- **Shoulders**: Align your shoulders directly above your sit bones. Soften the shoulders away from the ears.
- **Hands**: Place your hands gently on your knees or in a prayer position at your heart.
- **Gaze (Drishti)**: Look straight ahead or close your eyes.

Modifications
- **Using Props**: Place a blanket or bolster under your hips for added support. Place a block under the right knee if it's too elevated.
- **Alternative Pose**: If students' knees and shins do not stack comfortably, they may perform Sukhasana (Easy Seated Pose).

Contraindications and Risks
- Contraindicated for students with hip, knee, ankle, and foot injuries.

Easy Seated Twist | Parivrtta Sukhasana

pah-ree-vreet-tah soo-kah-sah-nah

Starting Position

Begin in Sukhasana (Crossed Leg Seated Pose).
Place your right hand on your left knee and your left hand behind you on the mat.
Twist, drawing your front ribs down as your sternum lifts.

Proper Alignment

- **Feet**: Flex your feet and stack them underneath the knees.
- **Legs**: Cross your left shin in front of your right shin.
- **Hips**: Stock your hips underneath your shoulders.
- **Torso**: Stack your head above your shoulders and your shoulders above your hips, keeping your spine vertically aligned from tail to stem. Lengthen through your spine, lifting through the crown of your head as you twist.
- **Hands**: Place your right hand on your left knee and your left hand behind you on the mat.
- **Neck**: Tuck your chin slightly in towards your chest to keep the back of your neck long. Lifting from the crown of the head.
- **Gaze (Drishti)**: Look over your left shoulder, keeping your neck long and relaxed.

Modifications

- **Using Props**: Students with lower back pain, tight hips, or sciatica are welcome to sit on a block or folded blanket to elevate their hips higher than their knees for support.

Contraindications and Risks

- **Specific Medical Needs**: Contraindicated for students with sciatica.

Half Lord of Fishes Pose I Ardha Matsyendrasana

ar-dha maht-see-en-drah-sah-nah

Starting Position

Begin sitting with your legs extended and your spine tall.

Bend your right knee and place your right foot outside your left thigh. Gently lean to your left side and bend your left knee, bringing your left foot near your right hip.

Sweep your left arm and lengthen through your left side, turning your chest toward your right knee.

Proper Alignment

- **Feet**: Place your right foot on the outside of your left thigh and your left foot near your right hip, keeping your feet relaxed.
- **Hips**: Firmly plant your sit bones to the mat as you sit up tall to maintain spinal length.
- **Torso**: Lengthen through your spine, lifting through the crown of your head as you twist.
- **Arms**: Sweep your left arm up and lengthen it through your left side. Then, bend your left elbow and place it outside the right knee.
- **Shoulders**: Roll your right shoulder down and back.
- **Hands**: Place your right hand a few inches behind your lower back.
- **Gaze (Drishti)**: Look over your right shoulder, keeping your neck long and relaxed.

Modifications

- **Using Props**: Students with lower back pain or spinal injuries should sit on a block or folded blanket to elevate their hips higher than their knees for support.

Contraindications and Risks

- **Back Pain**: Students with lower back pain or spinal injuries should exercise with caution. Keep your spine long and avoid rounding your back.

Pose Dedicated to the Sage Marichi I | Marichyasana I
mah-reech-yah-sah-nah

Starting Position
Begin in Dandasana (Staff Pose).
Bend your right knee and place your right foot flat on the mat, close to your right hip,
Bring your right arm to the inside of your right leg and reach both arms forward, lengthening evenly through the sides of your waist.
Wrap the right arm around the outer edge of the right leg and wrap the left arm behind the lower back. Interlace the fingers or clasp the hands.

Proper Alignment
- **Feet**: Keep your left leg extended and flex your left foot, with your left toes pointing straight to the sky to maintain a neutral rotation in your left hip. Place your right foot flat on the mat near your right hip and underneath your right knee.
- **Legs**: Engage your left quadriceps and inner thighs, pressing the back of your left leg into the mat, sensing the alignment and stability.
- **Hips**: Keep your hips in a neutral rotation.
- **Torso**: Fold slightly forward over your extended left leg.
- **Arms**: Reach both arms forward, lengthening evenly through both sides of the waist, and spin your palms away from each other. Wrap the right arm around the front of the right shin and reach the left arm back. Reach the right arm back.
- **Hands**: Interlace or clasp the hands.
- **Head**: Reach the center of the sternum forward and draw your forehead toward your extended shin.
- **Gaze (Drishti)**: Look down, keeping the back of your neck long and relaxed.

Modifications
- **Using Props**: Hold a strap between your hands if you cannot clasp them.

Pose Dedicated to the Sage Marichi III | Marichyasana III

mah-reech-yah-sah-nah

Starting Position

Begin in Dandasana (Staff Pose).

Bend your right knee and place your right foot flat on the mat, close to your right hip.

Lift your arms up to the sky to lengthen the spine.

Twist to the right, placing the left elbow outside the right knee and the proper fingertips behind you on the mat.

Proper Alignment

- **Feet**: Keep your left leg extended and flex your left foot, with your left toes pointing straight to the sky to maintain a neutral rotation in your left hip. Place your right foot flat on the mat near your right hip and underneath your right knee.
- **Legs**: Engage your left quadriceps and inner thighs, pressing the back of your left leg into the mat, sensing the alignment and stability.
- **Hips**: Keep your hips in a neutral rotation.
- **Torso**: Align your head above your shoulders and your shoulders above your hips. Lengthen through your spine, lifting through the crown of your head as you twist, feeling the openness and extension.

- **Arms:** Place your left elbow outside of your right knee and rest your right fingertips behind you on the mat.
- **Shoulder**: Roll your right shoulder back.
- **Hands**: Rest your right fingertips gently on the earth behind you. Option to bring the thumb and the index finger of the left hand together to connect for Gyan Mudra.
- **Gaze (Drishti)**: Look over your right shoulder or close your eyes, keeping your neck long and relaxed.

Modifications
- **Using Props**: Sit on a yoga block to elevate the hips higher than the legs.

Contraindications and Risks
- **Specific Medical Needs**: Contraindicated for students with high or low blood pressure.

279

Reclining Poses

Reclining poses, also known as supine poses, are primarily designed to promote relaxation. These poses allow the spine to be supported and rest while gently stretching various muscle groups, making them ideal for both beginners and advanced practitioners. Typically included at the end of a power yoga class, these poses help transition the body from vigorous activity to a restful state, preparing it for final relaxation in Savasana. They calm the nervous system, stretch muscles gently, correct spinal alignment, and aid in recovery.

All alignment instructions in this b are for the right side. Always repeat the same poses on the left side to maintain balance and promote symmetry and strength in your practice.

Knees to Chest Pose | Apanasana
ah-pah-nah-sah-nah

Starting Position
Begin lying on your back.
Draw both knees towards your chest, wrapping your arms around them.

Proper Alignment
- **Feet**: Keep your feet together.
- **Legs**: Draw your knees towards your chest and keep the inner edges of your legs connected.
- **Hips**: Press your tailbone towards the mat.
- **Torso**: Keep your back flat on the mat, lengthening through your spine.
- **Arms**: Wrap your arms around your shins, wrapping yourself in the warmest hug.
- **Hands**: Hold your shins, pressing gently to deepen the stretch.
- **Gaze (Drishti)**: Look straight up or close your eyes, keeping your neck long and relaxed.

Modifications
- **Using Props**: Consider placing a blanket under the neck for added support.
- **Alternating Poses**: Students with sensitive knees may hold the backs of their thighs behind the knees instead of grasping their shins.

Contraindications and Risks
- **Pregnancy**: Students who are pregnant and are still able to recline may consider widening the distance between their knees.

Single Knee to Chest Pose | Eka Pada Apanasana
ek-uh pah-duh ah-pah-nah-sah-nah

Starting Position
Begin in Knees to Chest Pose (Apanasana).
Extend your left leg onto the mat.
Draw your right knee towards your chest, extending your left leg on the mat.

Proper Alignment
- **Feet**: flex both feet slightly.
- **Legs**: Draw your right knee towards your chest.
- **Hips**: Rest your tailbone towards the mat.
- **Torso**: Keep your back flat on the mat, lengthening through your spine.
- **Hands**: Hold your right shin, pressing gently to deepen the stretch.
- **Gaze (Drishti)**: Look straight up or close your eyes, keeping your neck long and relaxed.

Modifications
- **Using Props**: Students with neck injuries or sensitivity may consider placing a folded blanket under their neck for added support.
- **Alternative Pose**: Students with sensitive knees may hold the back of their thigh behind the knee instead of grasping their shin.

Contraindications and Risks
- **Pregnancy**: Pregnant students who are still able to recline may draw their knee toward the shoulder rather than to the center of the chest.

Reclining Hand to Big Toe Pose | Supta Padangusthasana

soop-tah pah-duh-goose-tah-sah-nah

Starting Position
Begin lying on your back with your legs extended and your arms by your sides.
Wrap a strap around the sole of your right foot.
Extend the leg towards the right.

Proper Alignment
- **Feet**: Flex both feet and curl the toes towards the face.
- **Legs**: Engage your left quadriceps and inner thighs, pressing the back of your left leg into the mat. Your right leg should be extended towards the sky. Feel a stretch behind your right leg.
- **Hips**: Keep your hips level with each other and distribute your weight evenly on both hips. Press your tailbone towards the mat.
- **Torso**: Keep your back flat on the mat, lengthening through your spine.
- **Arms**: Extend your right arm, holding your strap or the right toe, and extend your left arm along the mat.
- **Hands**: Hold your strap to the right. Option to hook the big toe with the two-piece fingers of the right hand.
- **Gaze (Drishti):** Look straight up or towards your right foot or close your eyes, keeping your neck long and relaxed.

Reclining Pigeon I Thread the Needle Pigeon I

Starting Position
Begin in Apanasana (Knees to Chest Pose).
Place the soles of your feet flat on the floor with the feet hip-width apart.
Cross your right ankle over your left knee and actively flex your right foot.
Draw your left thigh toward your chest by interlacing your fingers behind your left thigh.

Proper Alignment
- **Feet**: Flex both feet to protect your knees and engage your leg muscles.
- **Legs**: Cross your right ankle over your left thigh, forming a figure four. Lift your left foot off the mat and draw your left knee towards your chest.
- **Hips**: Externally rotate through the right hip to open the knee to the front of your yoga mat. Keep your hips level with each other, and press your tailbone towards the mat, engaging your core. Avoid squeezing the knee with your hands.
- **Torso**: Keep your back flat on the mat, lengthening through your spine.
- **Arms**: Thread your right arm through the space between your legs and interlace your fingers behind your left thigh, wrapping it in towards your torso. Use your right elbow to draw the right thigh to the front of the yoga mat. To protect your knee, avoid placing your hands on your knees.
- **Shoulders**: Relax your shoulders down your back and broaden through your upper chest.
- **Hands**: Hug your left thigh in towards your chest, pressing gently to deepen the stretch.
- **Head**: Rest the back of your head on the mat and lengthen the crown of your head toward the back of the room.
- **Gaze (Drishti):** Look to the sky. Soften your gaze and keep your neck long and relaxed.

Modifications
- **Knee Pain**: Keep your left foot on the mat.

Contraindications and Risks
- **Pregnancy**: Contraindicated for students who are pregnant.

Happy Baby Pose | Ananda Balasana

ah-nahn-dah bah-lah-sah-nah

Starting Position

Begin in Apanasana (Knees to Chest Pose).
Place your hands on the outside edges of your feet and bring your arms toward the inner knees.

Proper Alignment

- **Feet**: Flex your feet, holding the outer edges with your hands.
- **Legs**: Bend your knees at a 90-degree angle, keeping them wider than your torso. Draw your knees towards the outer edge of your ribs, keeping your legs active and engaged.
- **Hips**: Press your tailbone towards the mat, lengthening your spine.
- **Torso**: Keep your entire spine flat on the mat, lengthening from the back of the head to the tailbone.
- **Arms**: Keep the elbows inside of the knees.
- **Hands**: Grip the outer edges of your feet.
- **Gaze (Drishti)**: Look straight up, keeping your neck long and relaxed.

Modifications

- **Adjustments**: Hold the backs of your knees or thighs instead of your feet.

Contraindications and Risks

- **Pregnancy**: Contraindicated for students who are pregnant. Proceed with caution.

Restorative Poses

Restorative poses in yoga are gentle, relaxing postures designed to promote deep relaxation and stress relief. These poses typically involve the use of props like blankets, bolsters, and blocks to support the body in a comfortable position, allowing for passive stretching and releasing tension. Restorative yoga helps activate the parasympathetic nervous system, inducing a state of calmness and promoting restorative rest.

All alignment instructions provided in this training are for the right side. In yoga practice, we often start with the right side, which is a tradition in many yoga classes. However, it is essential to always perform these poses on both sides to maintain balance in the body.

After completing the pose on the right side, please ensure you repeat the same pose on the left side, following the same alignment. Practicing on both sides will help you achieve a well-rounded and balanced practice, promoting symmetry and strength in your body.

Supine Bound Angle Pose | Salamba Supta Baddha Konasana

suh-lum-bah soop-tuh bah-dah cone-ah-sah-nah

Starting Position
- Begin lying on your back.
- Bring the soles of your feet together.
- Allow your knees to drop out to the sides.

Proper Alignment
- **Feet**: Bring the soles of your feet together.
- **Legs**: Allow your knees to fall out to the sides, forming a diamond shape with your legs.
- **Hips**: Rest your hips and tailbone on the earth. Keep your weight distributed evenly on both of your hips.
- **Torso**: Rest your spine on the earth beneath you, keeping the natural curves of the spine.
- **Arms**: Extend your arms by your sides, with the palms facing up. Keep a soft bending of the elbows and allow them to be supported by the earth beneath you.
- **Hands**: Option to place one hand on your heart and one hand on your belly for a nurturing touch.
- **Gaze**: Soften your gaze and close your eyes.

287

Modifications

- **Using Props - Supporting Your Base:** Place a bolster or two folded blankets lengthwise along the mat, bringing the base of the support a few inches away from your sacrum.
- **Using Props - Strap Your Waist:** Place a strap around the waist and loop it around the tops of the feet. Gently tighten the strap and draw the heels toward the body. Keep the metal part of the strap off your skin for comfort.
- **Using Props - Supporting Your Head:** Students may also wish to place a blanket under their heads for support.
- **Using Props - Supporting Your Knees:** Place blocks, rolled blankets, or smaller bolsters under your knees for support.

Contraindications and Risks

- There are no risks to this pose as long as the pose is fully supported.

Supported Bridge Pose | Salamba Setu Bandha Sarvangasana

suh-lum-bah say-too bun-duh sar-vun-gah-sah-nah

Starting Position

Begin reclining on your back with your knees bent and feet flat on the mat.
Press into your feet.
Lift your hips towards the sky, placing a yoga block horizontally under your sacrum.

Proper Alignment

- **Feet**: Keep your feet hip-width apart and parallel the big toes together like a number 11, making sure that your toes point straight ahead.
- **Legs**: Engage your inner thighs and hug them in towards the midline as if there was a yoga block between your inner thighs.
- **Hips**: Lift your hips off the mat, engaging your glutes and abdominal muscles, resting your sacrum on a bolster or a block at the lowest possible height. Ensure the long edge is perpendicular to the spine. Tuck your tailbone under and scoop your pelvis towards your face to lengthen the sacrum.
- **Torso**: Lengthen through your spine, lifting your chest towards your chin.
- **Shoulders**: tuck your shoulder blades slightly underneath to open the chest.
- **Arms**: Extend your arms along the mat, palms facing down, or clasp your hands under your back.
- **Gaze (Drishti)**: Look up towards the sky, keeping your neck long and relaxed.

Modifications

- **Using Props**: Students with a history of back pain may place a folded blanket for a lower height if it does not aggravate the pain.
- **Neck Problems**: Keep your gaze up and avoid turning your head to the side.

Contraindications and Risks

- **Special Medical Needs**: Contraindicated for people with herniated or bulged discs.

Legs up the Wall I Viparita Karani
vip-ah-ree-tah kah-rah-nee

Starting Position
Begin sitting with one side of your hip, pressing against the wall.
Sweep your legs up the wall.
Lower your back onto a yoga block horizontally at the lowest height.

Proper Alignment
- **Feet**: Extend your legs up the wall, flexing your feet slightly.
- **Legs**: Keep your legs straight.
- **Hips**: Rest your tailbone on a yoga block.
- **Torso**: Slightly scoop the pelvis toward the face.
- **Arms**: Extend your arms along the mat.
- **Shoulders**: Feel the shoulder blades being gently pressed by the earth.
- **Hands**: Spin your palms to face the sky.
- **Gaze (Drishti)**: Look straight up or close your eyes, keeping your neck neutral and relaxed.

Modifications
- **Using Props:** Students with neck pain may consider placing a blanket under their head to ensure proper support. Students with back pain may place a folded blanket under their hips for added support.

Contraindications and Risks
- **Neck pain:** Students with a history of neck pain should proceed cautiously and modify accordingly.

290

Supported Shoulder Stand I Salamba Sarvangasana

suh-lum-bah sar-vun-gah-sah-nah

Starting Position

Begin in Salamba Setu Bandha Sarvangasana (Supported Bridge Pose) with the yoga block horizontally at the lowest height.
Lift both legs toward the sky.

Proper Alignment

- **Feet**: Keep your legs together and extend them towards the sky, flexing your feet slightly.
- **Legs**: Keep your legs straight.
- **Hips**: Rest your tailbone on a yoga block.
- **Torso**: Slightly scoop the pelvis toward the face.
- **Arms**: Extend your arms along the mat.
- **Shoulders**: Feel the shoulder blades being gently pressed by the earth.
- **Hands**: Spin your palms to face the sky.
- **Gaze (Drishti):** Look straight up or close your eyes, keeping your neck neutral and relaxed.

Modifications

- **Using Props:** Students with neck pain may consider placing a blanket under their head to ensure proper support. Students with back pain may place a folded blanket under their hips for added support.

Contraindications and Risks

- **Neck pain:** Students with a history of neck pain should proceed cautiously and modify accordingly.

Corpse Pose | Savnsana

shah-vah-sah-nah

Starting Position

Begin lying on your back with your legs extended and your arms by your sides. Allow your body to relax, releasing tension.

Proper Alignment

- **Feet**: Let your feet fall naturally to the sides, keeping them relaxed.
- **Legs**: Extend your legs comfortably, allowing your hips to relax.
- **Hips**: Rest your tailbone towards the mat.
- **Torso**: Keep the natural curves in your spine.
- **Shoulders**: Slightly tuck your shoulder blades underneath you, allowing your chest to open.
- **Arms**: Extend your arms along the mat.
- **Hands**: Spin your palms up to face the sky, allowing your fingers to curl naturally.
- **Gaze (Drishti)**: Close your eyes, letting go of any tension in your face and jaw.

Modifications

- **Use Props**: Students may use a blanket to cover their body for warmth or place a folded blanket beneath their head for support. Students may also place a bolster under their knees to relieve their back muscles.

Inspirational Quotes

"Yoga is the journey of the self, through the self, to the self." - The Bhagavad Gita

"The body is your temple. Keep it pure and clean for the soul to reside in." - B.K.S. Iyengar

"Yoga is the practice of quieting the mind." - Patanjali

"The pose begins when you want to leave it." - Unknown

"Yoga is the dance of every cell with the music of every breath that creates inner serenity and harmony." - Debasish Mridha

"Yoga is the art of awareness on the canvas of body, mind, and soul." - Amit Ray

"Yoga is not about touching your toes, it's about what you learn on the way down." - Jigar Gor

"The rhythm of the body, the melody of the mind, and the harmony of the soul create the symphony of life." - B.K.S. Iyengar

"Yoga teaches us to cure what need not be endured and endure what cannot be cured." - B.K.S. Iyengar

"The journey of a thousand miles begins with one step." - Lao Tzu

"Nature does not hurry, yet everything is accomplished."- Lao Tzu

"Knowing others is intelligence; knowing yourself is true wisdom. Mastering others is strength; mastering yourself is true power." - Lao Tzu

"When I let go of what I am, I become what I might be." - Lao Tzu

"He who knows, does not speak. He who speaks, does not know." - Lao Tzu
"Silence is a source of great strength."- Lao Tzu

"Change the way you look at things and the things you look at change." - Dr. Wayne Dyer

"You cannot always control what goes on outside, but you can always control what goes on inside." - Dr. Wayne Dyer

"With everything that has happened to you, you can either feel sorry for yourself or treat what has happened as a gift. Everything is either an opportunity to grow or an obstacle to keep you from growing. You get to choose." - Dr. Wayne Dyer

"You'll see it when you believe it." - Dr. Wayne Dyer

"Walk as if you are kissing the Earth with your feet." - Thich Nhat Hanh

"To be beautiful means to be yourself. You don't need to be accepted by others. You need to accept yourself." - Thich Nhat Hanh

The Author

Maha Bodhi, M.A.

Maha Bodhi, M.A., is a globally recognized and celebrated yoga leader based in Malibu, CA. She is the creator and author of Yogi Maha Method and co-creator of The MINDRY Anywhere, a premiere mindfulness OnDemand app. Featured in the award winning HBO documentary "Scars Unseen", and alongside, Michelle Obama and Serena Williams, Maha Bodhi, M.A. is represented by the Harry Walker Agency in Beverly Hills, California.

Maha's Yoga Alliance school, Yogi Maha Method is the # 1 top rated Yoga Alliance school for training and certifying yoga instructors. Maha is an [E-RYT 500] and trained with celebrity yoga instructors Travis Eliot and Lauren Eckstrom.

School Lineage: Maha Bodhi => Travis Eliot => Srivatsa Ramaswami => B. K. S. Iyengar => Krishnamacharya."

Learn more about Maha at yogimaha.com

Book Designer & Editor

Tiffany Yau

Tiffany Yau is a researcher, social entrepreneur, best-selling author, and TEDx speaker who is passionate about equipping and empowering others with the needed resources and inspiration to make a positive impact on others, their community, and the world.

Tiffany is the founder of Fulphil, an education nonprofit that has empowered thousands of youths to build compassion and make an impact on their future careers by creating fun and engaging classroom education curricula. Recognized in Forbes, her TEDx talk, and several awards, Tiffany also founded several other successful social impact ventures, advised various nationally recognized mission-driven organizations, and published best-selling books, *Build With Impact* and *Speak Money*.

Tiffany is currently pursuing her Ph.D. in Strategy and Organizational Theory at the University of Southern California to study how businesses and individuals can effectively address grand societal and environmental challenges. She also holds a dual degree with high honors from the University of Pennsylvania, including an M.S. in Nonprofit Leadership and a B.A. in Sociology.

Index

A

B

Acknowledgments

This book would not have been possible without the incredible support and contributions of some truly talented individuals:

- **Tiffany Yau**: *I am deeply grateful for your design expertise, meticulous editing, and unwavering support in publishing this book. Your dedication ensured this vision became a reality. Additionally, thank you for stepping in and demonstrating some of the yoga poses with such elegance and grace.*

- **Isabel Simmons**: *Thank you for gracefully demonstrating many of the yoga poses featured throughout the book. Your presence brought these teachings to life.*

- **Gina Muscatel**: *A heartfelt thank you for generously allowing us to take the photos in your beautiful Malibu home. Your space added a serene and inspiring backdrop to the project.*

- **Raquel Anderson:** *Thank you for capturing the essence of each yoga pose with your photography. Your artistry beautifully highlights the heart of this practice.*

To all of you, I am forever grateful for your contributions, creativity, and belief in this project.